KINGFISHER CLASSICS

THE
ODYSSEY

Retold by Robin Lister

Illustrated by Alan Baker

Kingfisher Books

For my mother and father

Kingfisher Books, Grisewood & Dempsey Ltd,
Elsley House, 24-30 Great Titchfield Street,
London W1P 7AD

This reformatted edition published
by Kingfisher 1994
2 4 6 8 10 9 7 5 3 1
Originally published in hardback with colour
illustrations by Kingfisher 1987

BRITISH LIBRARY CATALOGUING IN PUBLICATION DATA
A catalogue record for this book is available
from the British Library

ISBN 1 85697 219 4

Printed and bound in Spain

THE
ODYSSEY

CONTENTS

SHIPWRECK

Alone in a small boat the sailor watched the rising sun splash crimson streaks across the sky and glisten on the still, dark surface of the Adriatic Sea. It was a lovely Mediterranean dawn, but the sailor had no time to linger over the beauty of a sight he had seen a thousand times before. Instead, his sleepless eyes gazed anxiously at the horizon, straining to see.

As the sun rose higher and the day brightened the sailor began to make out dark shapes in the distance. At first they looked like clouds. Then, as the boat slowly drew closer, he saw that they were hills. His heart leapt and beat faster. A fresh wind filled his sails and blew his craft forward. Soon he could make out clusters of trees on the lower slopes of the hills and, beneath them, jagged rocks, which appeared to float on the blue-black sea. Now, in spite of the distance, the sailor knew that these were the cliffs and mountains of Ithaca, his island home. Beloved, long-lost Ithaca.

At once the weariness of seventeen sleepless days and nights alone at sea dissolved, forgotten. Tears of joy streamed down the sailor's salt-lined

face into his black beard. After twenty long years of war, wandering and captivity, he, Odysseus, was coming home.

But he had thanked the gods too soon. The storm appeared from the south and struck without warning. Black clouds massed overhead, thunder cracked and lightning snaked across the sky. A fierce tempest whipped up the sea so suddenly that there was no time to haul in the sail. Odysseus clung helplessly to the rudder as his boat was tossed from wave to wave. The mast snapped, narrowly missing him as it fell. In the next instant an enormous wave crashed across the deck and swept him out into the angry sea. By the time he had struggled, breathless, to the surface, his boat was nowhere to be seen.

Odysseus found himself floating next to the broken mast. He grabbed hold of it and lashed himself to it with his belt. As he did so a giant wave swelled up from the seething water and towered over him. He looked up at the arching crest in terror. Poseidon, god of the sea, stared angrily down at him, brandishing his great trident. Then the wave crashed down; and everything went black. At once the skies cleared. The wind dropped. The storm was over, Odysseus left for dead.

But he was not dead. Although he was battered, unconscious and half-drowned, the mast kept him afloat as he drifted, oblivious, away from the shores of his long-lost kingdom.

Hours later he came to, bruised, sore and so weak that he could barely lift his head to look around. In every direction the sea stretched away empty to the horizon. He was utterly lost. Just when it seemed that his prayers had been answered and Ithaca was in sight, fate had played its cruellest trick. The gods would have been far kinder to let him die years ago, hundreds of miles from home.

Overcome with grief he buried his face in his arms. Great sobs of despair welled up from his heart. He did not see the seagull settle on his mast and change into the shape of a beautiful woman. It was the sea-nymph Ino. Odysseus looked up, astonished, when she spoke to him in a voice half-human, half-divine.

"Poor Odysseus, what have you done to make Poseidon so angry? You may have survived the storm but, without my help, you will drift round and round under the scorching sun until you wish you had never been born. Your only hope of reaching land alive is to swim with the currents. I will give you an enchanted scarf which will protect you and keep you afloat when you are too tired to swim. As soon as you come ashore you must throw it back into the sea."

The sea-nymph slipped the scarf from her waist and gently tied it round Odysseus. Then, changing back into a seagull, she spread her wings and flew on her way.

Odysseus gazed after her. Bitter experience had taught him to trust no one, especially the gods. Perhaps Poseidon had sent her to trick him? But he had little choice. If he clung to the mast he would surely drift to a slow, agonizing death under the burning sun.

The salt water had shrunk his belt, making it difficult to untie. He worked at it patiently until it came loose. Then he stripped off his clothes, fastened the sea-nymph's scarf firmly back round his waist and began to swim.

For two days and two nights he swam with the currents. Often he had to rest, letting the current carry him along. At last, at dawn on the third day, he came in sight of land. It was late afternoon before he finally dragged himself ashore, faint with exhaustion.

He lay for a long time on the smooth pebbles, unable to move. When he found the strength to look around, he saw that the beach was in a small inlet where a stream flowed out into the sea. He carefully untied Ino's scarf and dropped it into the clear running water, then knelt down and began to drink from the stream.

As he drank he began to shiver. Night was falling fast and he had to find shelter quickly. If he stayed on the beach, naked and exposed, he might not survive the night. He climbed up from the beach, keeping to the bank of the stream, until he came to a dense copse. There he found two bushy olives which had grown into one another to form a natural shelter. Gathering up armfuls of leaves, he spread them on the ground for comfort and warmth. Then he collapsed into his makeshift bed with the soothing song of the stream in his ears and sank into a deep sleep.

NAUSICAA

Odysseus was dreaming. It was a nightmare that he knew all too well. He was back in the wooden horse with his comrades, Menelaus, Diomedes and the rest. They were sick with fear, dry-mouthed, shivering and drenched in sweat, just as they had been in reality when the Trojans dragged the great horse across the plain from the Greek camp to their lovely city. Only in the nightmare, instead of dragging the horse into Troy as the Greeks had intended, the Trojans hauled it up onto the cliffs and pushed it over the edge. Then it was falling; falling, it seemed for ever, down onto the rocks below. Odysseus cried out in terror.

He woke suddenly, in a cold sweat. For a moment he thought another nightmare had begun. Everywhere he looked he saw eyes staring at him and he froze, like an animal startled in its lair. As his own eyes adjusted to the dim light, he was amazed to see a group of young women peering into his shelter. Before he could move, they turned and ran off through the trees. All except one. Although she was trembling, the tallest of the girls stood her ground and stared back at Odysseus

with proud, unblinking eyes.

The girl watched Odysseus crawl out of his shelter and stand before her like some wild amphibian creature. He was naked, his unkempt hair and beard bedraggled and encrusted, like his skin, with salt, seaweed and dead leaves. The girl was radiantly beautiful. The two of them stared at one another in amazement before Odysseus spoke.

"Are you a vision or are you real? You must be a princess or even a goddess. You remind me of Artemis the huntress, daughter of mighty Zeus. Are those young women who ran away the nymphs who keep you company?" The girl smiled at this idea as Odysseus continued.

"Whoever you are, I need your help. You see before you an unlucky wanderer, desperate to return to his family and home. Let me tell you how I come to be here, naked and alone, a stranger in a strange land." Odysseus then recounted the story of his ordeal at sea. As she listened, the girl was unable to take her eyes off the deep bruises which covered his body. It was a miracle that he had survived.

"Poor unlucky man, how you have suffered! But now your luck has changed, for here you will find all the help you need. I am Nausicaa; this land is Phaeacia and my father, Alcinous, the king. Come," she said, stretching out a lovely hand, "we must find you some clothes and something to eat. Then I'll take you to my father's palace."

And, taking him gently by the hand, Nausicaa led Odysseus out of the wood.

The young women were waiting nervously at the edge of the copse. At the sight of Odysseus they started back again.

"What a sorry lot you are!" Nausicaa laughed, tossing back her mane of black hair. "Anyone would think you'd never seen a man before."

Once they were sure that Odysseus was indeed a man and not some savage beast or spirit of the woods, the young women began to laugh at themselves too. Nausicaa told one of them to fetch him some clothes from the laundry-wagon which stood by the stream, while she herself prepared a meal. The girls' half-eaten picnic lay in the shade of the ancient olive, exactly as they had left it when they heard the strange cry from the copse. Meanwhile Odysseus plunged into the clear stream and washed the brine and grime from his skin and hair. When he was clean, he dried in the sun and rubbed olive oil into his chapped, bruised skin. Then he wrapped himself in a white and purple tunic which Arete, Nausicaa's mother, had woven.

The girls were astonished to see the terrifying savage transformed into the god-like creature who now sat beneath the olive tree by the water. They watched, fascinated, as he ate and drank slowly and delicately, in spite of his ravenous hunger. "This man is close to the gods," thought Nausicaa. "With such a man I would gladly share my life."

Odysseus sensed that he was being watched and looked up to see the young princess staring at him. She blushed at the thought that he might be reading her mind and he quickly looked away, not wishing to embarrass her.

By the time he had finished eating, the young women had rounded up their mules and harnessed them to the wagon. Nausicaa took the reins.

"Noble stranger," she called to Odysseus, "it's time to go now. Walk along with us and I'll take you to my father's palace."

The girls laughed and sang as they climbed up through the meadows towards the town. They often glanced at the stranger in their midst – they could not help it – but Odysseus did not notice. He was too busy wondering what lay in store for him at the palace and, as he walked along, he sent up a silent prayer to his guardian goddess Athene, daughter of mighty Zeus.

They were soon at the city walls and passed through the gates. It was a beautiful town of whitewashed houses, decked with pots of geraniums, vines, climbing roses and sweet-smelling rosemary. At the centre lay the harbour, where rows of magnificent ships were moored. Alongside the harbour was the assembly-place and above this stood the palace. They entered a courtyard studded with fabulous mosaics and arrayed with statues and ornamental pools and fountains. On either side of the courtyard were sumptuous gardens, full of herbs, fruits and flowers, dominated by great cedars of Lebanon. It was a glorious sight. Odysseus looked around with admiration as he followed the princess to the golden doors of the palace itself.

Now Nausicaa and Odysseus went on alone. They climbed the steps between fierce-faced gold and silver watchdogs, which reminded Odysseus of three-headed Cerberus, the dreadful dog that guards the gates of Hades. At the top of the steps he took a deep breath, then followed Nausicaa across the bronze threshold into the great hall.

THE
UNEXPECTED
GUEST

A hush fell over the great hall as they entered. The Phaeacian lords were amazed. Who on earth could this stranger be and what was he doing with Nausicaa? Ignoring their stares, the princess led Odysseus past the long banqueting table to the far end of the hall, where her father and mother sat before the fire. Nausicaa explained how she found him and repeated the story of his shipwreck and his longing to return home. When she had finished the king stayed silent.

It was Nausicaa's mother, silver-haired Arete, who spoke. "You are welcome to Phaeacia, dear stranger, and we're only sorry that it's misfortune which has brought you here. We'll do all we can to help you return to your home and family. But now I'm curious to know who you are and where you come from.

18

It isn't every day that an unexpected guest comes to Phaeacia."

"Wise Arete, your words are most gracious," replied Odysseus, still kneeling in the ashes of the hearth. "I hope you'll understand if I don't answer your questions now. Since shipwreck has brought me to your beautiful land with nothing but my life, I can offer nothing but words as proof of who I am. When I tell you, you'll be astonished. At first you may not believe me, although as my story unfolds you'll realize that I know too much to have made it up. But my story is long as my suffering has been great and I am too weary to tell you now."

"Of course, of course," put in King Alcinous before his wife could reply. "We must let you rest before we ask you to do any explaining. And it's not right," he continued, getting up from his seat by the fire, "that you should kneel there in the ashes while we all stare at you open-mouthed as though you were a creature from another world. It doesn't matter whether you're the poorest beggar or one of the great gods in disguise, you're our

19

guest and hospitality demands that we should make all guests feel at home."

With these words the king helped Odysseus to his feet and led him to the centre of the great banqueting table where his favourite son, Laodamas, was sitting. Laodamas got up at once and gracefully offered the stranger his seat.

"Now eat and drink your fill," said Alcinous. "Afterwards my daughter's maids will show you to your bed. Tomorrow we'll entertain you and arrange your journey home."

Later that night, alone in his bed, Odysseus prayed once more to his guardian goddess, Athene. Surely now he was as good as home.

When Alcinous came to rouse his unknown guest the following dawn he found him already dressed, gazing at the reddening sky. He was trying to imagine the same sun rising over Ithaca.

The king brought good news. A ship was being prepared to carry Odysseus home and a crew of fifty-two of Phaeacia's finest young oarsmen had volunteered to take him. They would be ready to sail that evening. Odysseus was overjoyed. Meanwhile there was to be the entertainment which Alcinous had promised.

After a quick breakfast of bread and wine, the king led his guest to the assembly-place in front of the palace. Here the best runners and fighters in Phaeacia had gathered to show off their athletic skills.

Odysseus could think of the journey home and nothing else. Nevertheless, out of consideration for his hosts, he pretended to enjoy the spectacle and applauded each of the winners with apparent enthusiasm. When the games were over Prince Laodamas, the champion boxer, came up to him and invited him to challenge one of the winners in whichever event he pleased.

"Dear prince," replied Odysseus, "You will have to forgive me for I have no heart for games today."

"No, no, of course not. I understand."

"And I certainly understand, dear stranger," sneered Euryalus, the champion discus thrower, who in form and beauty looked like Ares, son of great Zeus and god of war. "You're not in the mood for games because you're scared of making a fool of yourself. I bet the only games that you're any good at are the ones you make money from. You might have the body of an athlete, but you've got the heart of a merchant. You've probably never thrown a discus or strung a bow in your life, yet here you are mysteriously posing as someone noble and important."

White with anger, Odysseus rose from his seat. "Foolish, insolent boy, I see whoever made you forgot to give you brains and whoever brought you up forgot to teach you manners. I long for my home and my mind is filled by many years of sorrow. How could I think of playing games? The tiniest drop of wisdom would have told you that. But since you've insulted me with such ill-chosen words I shall teach you a lesson."

And, without bothering to remove his cloak, Odysseus picked up a discus, which was larger and heavier than any the Phaeacians had used. He spun round expertly on his feet to gain momentum, and let it go. He was still weak and stiff after his ordeal at sea, but the goddess Athene was watching over him and gave him renewed strength. The discus flew far beyond the earlier throws. Gasps of amazement went round the assembly-place, followed by murmurs of admiration.

There were no further challenges. As they made their way back to the palace, where a huge feast had been prepared, the Phaeacians looked at their unknown guest with even greater interest than before; now their interest was mingled with deep respect. More than ever they wondered who their visitor could be.

Alcinous had promised that Odysseus would be entertained and he was as good as his word. Twelve sheep, eight wild boar and two oxen had been slaughtered, dressed and roasted; huge jars of the best Phaeacian wine had been brought up from the cellar.

When his guests were all seated and served, Alcinous had his favourite bard, Demodocus, brought out to sing to them. Watching the frail, blind old man led to a seat in the middle of the hall, Odysseus found it hard to believe that he could still perform. Surely his ancient voice would sound cracked and feeble? And how could those arthritic fingers pluck the strings of the lyre? Yet as soon as Demodocus sounded the first notes and opened his mouth to sing, the Ithacan knew that he was listening to the music of the gods. Although he had no appetite for the feast, sick as he was with longing for home, Odysseus entirely forgot himself in the Olympian music.

Demodocus sang first of the love of Ares, god of war, and Aphrodite, goddess of love, and of the anger and revenge of Aphrodite's husband, Hephaestus, god of fire and forge. The song was funny and moving by turns and when it was over Odysseus led the applause. Then Demodocus began a second song, this time a song of the Trojan war, about the famous quarrel of Odysseus and Achilles. It was painful for Odysseus even to think of those years of war and his lost comrades. As he listened to the lovely, melancholy song, he was overcome and covered his face with his hands to hide his tears.

Alcinous saw his mysterious guest's distress and a question stirred in his mind. However, he said nothing and, when Demodocus had finished and the applause had died away, he ordered the dancers to take the floor. To the rhythm of drums and chants, while blind Demodocus plucked his lyre, the young men and women of Phaeacia, led by Nausicaa and Laodamas, swayed, leapt and spun before him. Roused from his misery, Odysseus was dazzled by the display, and lost no time in praising the dancers. The king was delighted.

"Listen, my friends, to how well our mysterious guest has appreciated our music and our dance. Now, before we ask him to tell us his story, let's shower him with gifts so that wherever he goes he'll speak well of Phaeacia. And you, Euryalus, should be the first to come forward."

Without hesitation Euryalus rose from his place and turned to Odysseus. He unbuckled his sword and held it out in both hands. "Dear stranger, please accept this token and forgive my foolish insults. I beg you to remember the giver of the gift and not the arrogant young fool who abused you. Treasure the sword well. It's made of fine bronze and the hilt is pure silver. You can see its beauty for yourself."

Odysseus took the sword and placed a hand on the young man's shoulders. "Euryalus, you've apologized most gracefully. I'll remember you as you wish and may the gods bless your life."

After Euryalus, the twelve Phaeacian princes of rank brought their gifts forward and Odysseus was soon surrounded by treasures. He was delighted. Having lost all the riches which he had plundered from Troy, at least he would not now be returning home empty-handed. When his gifts had been stowed in a vast chest and carried off to the ship, Odysseus poured out a glass of the best wine and carried it to Demodocus. Silence fell as he knelt down before the withered old man.

"Demodocus, I offer you this as a sign of my admiration. All poets and musicians deserve our praise because they sing of human suffering and joy, explain us to ourselves and teach us to understand our world. But I praise you above all men because your voice is god-like and your music more beautiful than any I've heard."

He handed the glass to the blind old man who took it in a shaking hand. "I must ask you one last favour," said Odysseus. "Earlier you sang of the quarrel between the great Achaean lords, Odysseus and Achilles. I would like you to sing of the Achaeans once more but of a later theme. Sing to us now of the wooden horse which enabled the Greeks at last, after ten long, weary years, to enter Troy and destroy it."

Demodocus beamed with pleasure as Odysseus praised him. Now he raised his glass towards the Ithacan's voice and drained it with the vigour of a young man. He then set down the glass, plucked at his lyre and began to sing.

DEMODOCUS SINGS OF THE WOODEN HORSE

For ten long years the Greeks laid siege to Troy and for ten long years the Trojans resisted. For ten long years the Greeks had been away from their homes and families and many of the bravest among them had died in battle. And why had they endured these ten years of hardship and bitter loss? Why, because of nothing more than hurt pride. Lovely Helen, daughter of mighty Zeus and wife of King Menelaus of Sparta, had run off to Troy with Paris, the Trojan prince. For ten years the Greeks had been fighting to win her back.

Many of the Greeks had begun to question the sense of carrying on. It seemed crazy to give up so much for such a small matter of pride. Morale was low and their hearts were turning to home, where their families would be growing old without them. At the same time it seemed a dreadful waste to give up the fight and return home empty-handed after so many years. So it was that they decided to try cunning where brute force had failed.

It was Odysseus who thought up the idea. With Athene's help, the Greek carpenter Epeius built an enormous wooden horse. It was as high as a house with a huge hollow belly. Odysseus and selected comrades climbed inside, armed to the teeth. Then they pulled shut the small trap-door which was invisible from the outside. Once they were inside the rest of the Greeks dismantled their camp, boarded their ships and sailed away from Troy. It seemed the siege was over.

So the Trojans thought. They watched the last of the Greek ships disappear over the horizon, then threw open the gates of their city and descended on the Greek camp in triumph. At first they were not sure what to make of the enormous wooden horse. There were those who distrusted the Greeks entirely and thought it must be a booby-trap. They argued that they should burn it or hurl it over the cliffs but they were shouted down amid the noisy celebrations. Nevertheless, it was a nerve-wracking time for the men inside.

The Trojans attached strong ropes to the horse and dragged it back to their city as a prize of war. Whenever they stopped the Greeks inside fell over each other with a clang and clatter of armour and swords. They were sure their enemies must have heard them, but the Trojans heard nothing above

the sound of their songs and chants. Finally the Trojans dragged the horse to the temple in the middle of their city, intending to offer it to the gods in gratitude for their victory. It proved to be a fateful offering.

That night, when the city was deep in sleep after its joyous celebrations, Odysseus and his comrades slid down from the horse on a rope and silently killed the sentinels, who lay in a drunken stupor along the city walls. At the same time the Greek fleet, which had been at anchor on the far side of the island of Tenedos, just off the coast, had returned to the Trojan shores under cover of darkness. Odysseus and his men threw open the city gates to let in the main army and the wholesale slaughter and burning began. The Greeks overcame all resistance by surprise and took their revenge without mercy. Bloody corpses soon lay heaped up on the streets and the night sky over the city was lit up by the blazing flames which devoured its buildings.

Odysseus, with Menelaus at his side, led the assault on Deiphobus' palace where Helen was housed. They killed Deiphobus and all the guards, seized the lovely Helen, ransacked the palace and set it alight. White-haired Priam, venerable king of Troy, was butchered on the altar by Neoptolemus, Achilles' son. Everywhere terror and destruction reigned. The Greeks carried away all the riches of Troy, leaving behind only rubble and ashes.

And Helen, the cause of so much bloodshed and bitter loss, returned to Sparta in triumph with her husband Menelaus; there she is served by Trojan slaves and feasts on the spoils of war.

As for the rest, their stories are all told. Some, like old Nestor, Neptolemus and Menelaus himself, are back in their kingdoms enjoying the fruits of war in peace. Others, like Agamemnon, brother of Menelaus and overlord of all Greece, returned home only to meet with dreadful death. Others still perished on the sea. Only Odysseus is unaccounted for. There are rumours of his death and even a tale that he is imprisoned on Calypso's enchanted isle. Who can tell which is the truth? Even today the fate of Odysseus, wisest and bravest of all the Greeks, remains unknown and may remain hidden until the end of time.

So Demodocus sang, as Odysseus had requested, and his song was so beautiful and his subject so terrible that when he had finished his audience stayed silent, on the verge of tears. For who could listen to such lovely music and hear of the death of white-haired Priam and not be deeply moved? But for Odysseus himself the song was too painful to bear. It brought back vivid memories of dear, lost comrades and sights so horrible that he had chosen to forget them. Tears streamed from his eyes while Demodocus sang and again Alcinous saw the intense effect of the song on his mysterious guest.

"Fellow Phaeacians," said the king, in the hush which followed the song, "I see that our guest is lost in sorrow. When Demodocus sang earlier of the quarrel between Odysseus and Achilles, I saw how sad he was to hear it." Here Alcinous turned to Odysseus and placed a fatherly hand on his shoulder: "Dear guest and stranger, we've given you the best of everything we have and we've prepared a fine ship to carry you home. All I ask in return is that you now tell us your story as you promised last night. Who are you, where do you come from and where have you been wandering these past twenty years? And why are you so stirred by songs of Troy? Did you lose some close relative or dear friend there?"

Odysseus listened to the barrage of questions and stared at the ground. He could barely bring himself to speak. His story held so many bitter memories, told of so much loss. There was a long pause, during which neither a throat cleared nor a chair scraped, before he looked up and surveyed his audience. At last, taking several deep breaths and fighting back his tears, Odysseus spoke. "Dear, good Alcinous, you've been more than gracious. You've taken me in and trusted me, you've fed me, clothed me and entertained me royally, you've provided a ship to carry me home. Now you ask me to open my heart and tell my story and I shall do so, although it's a long story, full of misery and grief." Odysseus paused and took a long draught from the cup of wine at his side. "I am Odysseus, son of Laertes, and Ithaca – lovely, brave, rugged Ithaca – is my home. I am Odysseus of whom Demodocus sang, that same Odysseus who rescued Helen and who set sail for home in triumph after ten long years of war. Of the Trojan war enough has already been said. It's a story that everyone knows. I shall tell you my own story, the story of my wanderings, of the ten years that I've spent trying to get home."

THE CYCLOPS

After ten years in a hot overcrowded army camp no one was sorry to leave. The different sectors of the Greek army said their goodbyes, wished one another swift and successful voyages and cast off from Trojan shores for the last time. In our small fleet of twelve ships I and my Ithacan followers set our course for home. We were exultant. Instead of the stifling heat of the dusty plains, we had a fresh sea-breeze on our cheeks and the salt spray tasted of long forgotten pleasures, making us ache with joy. Our crimson ships were filled with the riches of Troy and we were glad that we would have so much to show for our long absence. Behind us Troy lay smoking in ruins. Perhaps it was superstition, but not one of us looked back. No, no, we all looked forward towards Ithaca, towards our home.

The wind, however, was south-south-east and we were driven northwards to the land of the Cicones. No doubt still flushed by our success at Troy, we disembarked and swept through the town of Ismarus, seizing whatever took our fancy and killing whoever stood in our way. It was sheer piracy, an orgy of looting, but my men wanted to carry home as much wealth as possible. Besides, after four days at sea, it was sensible to replenish our diminishing stores of food and wine.

As soon as we had pillaged the town I ordered our getaway. Unfortunately, my men had already grown complacent, fat on their success. They laughed at me and told me to relax and enjoy myself, because that is what they were going to do. So we spent that evening on the shores of Ismarus in drunken celebration, roasting whole oxen and sheep and drinking vast quantities of strong red wine.

Just as I feared, the Cicones had gone inland in search of reinforcements to drive away their unwelcome visitors. They attacked our camp at dawn. You can imagine our condition. Our famous army was overwhelmed and driven back onto the beach where the ships were moored. We were lucky to get away with out losing more than about six men (out of sixty) from each ship.

We were glad to escape so lightly, but we were saddened by the loss of our comrades. It seemed an unnecessary waste and indeed it was. Besides, it now dawned on us that we were still a long way from home and, if the gods were against us, that we might never get there. The exuberant mood in which we sailed away from the coast of Troy had gone for good.

As though to confirm our new sense of foreboding a violent storm blew up. We managed to lower our sails and row into the shore before any damage was done. There followed two anxious days in which we watched the tempest churn up the sea. On the third day we were able to cast off once more and we now made rapid progress south. Within a week we reached Maleia, the south-east cape of the Peloponnese, and our confidence began to return. But as we rounded the cape, ready for the last leg of our journey north towards Ithaca, a gale-force wind blew up from the east and drove us off course, past Cythera and miles to the west.

For nine days the wind blew us westwards, further and further from home. We could only sit by helplessly and watch. On the tenth day we were blown onto the shores of Libya. We disembarked and some of us went in search of water while others prepared a meal. After we had eaten and begun to recover, sent a small party off to spy out the land and see what they could find out about its inhabitants. Meanwhile the rest of us set about the task of cleaning up our ships and repairing their damaged sails.

It was not long before we were ready to sail once more, but my party of explorers had not returned. We waited and waited and still there was no sign of them. In the end I had no choice but to send out a second party in search of the first and, when this second lot failed to return, I decided to go and look for them myself. I took half a dozen of my most reliable men and, together, we climbed the cliffs above the beach and made our way inland.

It did not take long to find them. They had met with some natives of that land who had made them welcome and given them lotus fruit to eat. The lotus fruit, so my men told me afterwards, tastes of nectar and honeydew and is so strong a drug that whoever eats it is instantly addicted. Once my men had tasted it they lost all desire to return home and wished only to remain forever in the land of the Lotus-Eaters, feasting on this strange and dangerous fruit.

Although the drug made them too drowsy to put up much resistance, it took a great effort to drag them all back to the ships. Ignoring their tears and pleas to be left behind, we bound them with ropes and shoved them in the hold of my ship until we had sailed away far from the Libyan coast.

Now we were despondent. As far as we knew we were further than ever from home but, worse still, we were no longer sure how to get there. That night we came to a small wooded island lying close to a much larger one. Here we found a sandy inlet where we ran our ships up on the beach and made our camp. As soon as we began to explore our new surroundings we thought that our luck had turned. The island's only inhabitants were abundant flocks of goats and it was not long before we had caught a hundred or so and set about preparing a feast. Later, as we lay under the stars on the soft sand, savouring the delicious wine, of which we still had plenty, we noticed the glow of fires on the large island nearby. We also heard the bleating of sheep and goats and, from time to time, unmistakably human shouts.

It struck us as odd that people should live so close and yet not use the small island on which we had camped. The flocks of wild goats were matched by good soil, luxuriant vegetation and sweet-tasting natural springs. The thought that the island held some hideous secret made us uneasy as we prepared to sleep but we resolved to sail across to the larger island the next day. This was not a matter of idle curiosity. We wanted to find out where we were and get directions for our journey.

The following day was heralded by one of those lovely Mediterranean dawns which gladden the heart. Leaving the main body of the fleet where it was, I sailed across to the mainland with my crew. We moored our ship in a small natural harbour and, together with twelve of my crew, I clambered ashore. We had not gone far when we came to the entrance of a great cave covered in laurels. Walls of stone and timber formed a courtyard in front of it. Getting no response to our cries of greeting, we decided to investigate the cave for ourselves.

It was dim inside, but pleasantly cool and airy and, as soon as our eyes had adjusted to the light,

we saw pens full of lambs and kids. Alongside these stood buckets of whey in rows and baskets of cheese stacked high, right up to the ceiling.

"Whoever lives here must be a giant," I joked as I looked around. "Anyone else would need a ladder to get to the top of those stacks and there's no ladder here."

My men were all for taking as many cheeses, lambs and kids as we could and making our escape before the owner returned. I was outraged.

"We're not mean, sneaking burglars but men of honour!" I exclaimed. "Besides, unless we wait for the owner, how do we find out where we are?"

This shamed them into silence. We lit a fire and helped ourselves to some of the excellent cheese while we waited.

We did not have to wait long. As soon as we saw the owner I realized that it had been a terrible mistake to stay. He was not merely a giant, he was a colossus, with an ugly, savage face and a single, huge eye planted right in the middle of his forehead.

He penned up his rams and billy-goats in the courtyard and drove his ewes and milking-goats inside. When he had sealed up the entrance to the cave with an enormous boulder that twenty strong men could not have shifted, he set about milking his flocks and curdling some of the milk to make cheese. Once he had finished, he rekindled the fire, ready to eat his supper and settle down for the night.

All this while we had cowered in the shadows, hoping by some miracle to escape his notice. But as soon as the firelight spread about the cave he saw us, his uninvited guests. "Who the hell are you?" he growled. "And what are you doing here?"

We were terrified and I had to make a great effort to sound calm as I replied. "We are Greeks lost at sea on our return from Troy. We come to you in the hope that you'll help us find our way and, in the name of mighty Zeus, patron of all guests and suppliants, we ask you to show us your hospitality."

The giant bared his foul teeth and laughed in my face. "You can forget your mighty Zeus, little Greek. I'm a Cyclops and we Cyclops couldn't care less about the gods. As for my hospitality, you'll have a chance to sample that in a moment. But first tell me more. Where have you moored your ship and how many other little Greeks did you leave behind to guard it?"

"Our ship was broken up on the rocks," I replied, thinking quickly. "We are the only survivors."

The Cyclops grunted and spat in the dust at my feet. Then, without warning, he seized two of my companions and smashed their heads against the rock walls of the cave until their blood ran down and soaked into the floor. Before our sickened eyes he devoured them whole and, smacking his bulbous lips, washed down his last mouthfuls with two buckets of milk. We huddled in a corner, too shocked and disgusted to speak, as the Cyclops lay down among his animals and slept.

I drew my sword with a trembling hand, ready to kill him then and there. But to do so would have been suicide, for we could never have shifted the enormous boulder which sealed the door.

We passed a wretched night, pressed together for comfort, unable to sleep. Next morning the Cyclops rekindled the fire, milked his flocks and ate two more of my companions for breakfast. Then, having shut us in, he drove his flocks off to the mountain-side and left us in despair. We had to do something quickly or in another two days this gruesome creature would have consumed us all. But what on earth could we do? I thought and I thought until at last I came up with a scheme.

Alongside the pens lay a long trunk of olive, the size of a mast on one of our ships. I cut off a length, sharpened it to a point and, because it was still green, set it to harden in the fire. When I was satisfied with my work, I hid the weapon under the layers of dung which lay about the cave. Too anxious to talk or eat, we waited for the monster to return.

He came at nightfall, driving his flocks before him into the cave. Perhaps he sensed that he was at risk, perhaps some god had warned him, I don't know, but this time he didn't leave a single ram or billy-goat out in the fenced court yard. When all the animals were inside, he rolled the massive boulder back into place and set about milking his flocks as before. He put the lambs and kids to their mothers, set some of the milk to curdle, then grabbed two more of my men and made his bloody meal of them. He was still belching and spitting out their bones when I decided to put my plan into action. There was no time to lose.

I had with me a skin of the dark, fragrant wine which Maron, priest of Apollo at Ismarus, had given me because I protected him and his family from the brutality of my men. This was special wine, a drink for the gods, with a heady fragrance which made it irresistible. Maron would mix it with twenty parts of spring-water when he offered it to his friends and one glass was still enough to make them drunk.

I filled a bowl to the brim with the undiluted wine and carried it over to the Cyclops.

"Pitiless Cyclops," I began, terrified that he would devour me then and there, "surely you've had your fill of human meat? You've eaten six of my men and there are only seven of us left. I had intended to offer you this wine in return for your hospitality. Now I can only hope that its divine fragrance will soften your heart and turn your thoughts to mercy."

The grinning monster grabbed the bowl and swallowed the wine in a single gulp. He belched noisily and demanded another, which he drank off like the first. His grin slackened and he belched again, then smacked his fleshy lips and rubbed his vast stomach.

"Well, well, well, little Greek, you've managed to surprise me. We Cyclops make good wine but this is in a different class. Give me some more and tell me your name. In return for your excellent wine

I'm going to do you a special favour."

The Cyclops let out an evil chuckle. He slapped his sides and roared with laughter so that the cave echoed and the flocks shifted uneasily in their pens. The wine was having its effect. The Cyclops drank three more bowls in quick succession. His grin became a drunken leer and when he spoke again he slurred his words. "Come on then, little Greek, I asked you your name. Out with it, no need to be shy."

To humour the monster I tried to sound as meek as possible, which under the circumstances was only too easy. "Mighty Cyclops, my name is Noman. Now I beg you to grant me the favour you promised me."

"Well, Noman, this is what I'm going to do. I'll put you at the bottom of the menu and eat all your friends first. That way you you'll be able to enjoy my hospitality a little longer."

And with a final belch and a braying laugh the monster slumped into a drunken stupor and began to snore.

At once I pulled the wooden stake from its hiding-place and thrust it into the embers of the fire. Within minutes it was glowing red-hot. Trembling with fear, we carried it over to where the sleeping giant lay flat on his back and raised it above his head. I gave the word, "Now!" and my men drove the stake down into the monster's single eye, while I hung from the top to give it greater force.

There was a loud hiss as the burning wood pierced the watery membrane. The eye steamed for a moment, then the blood gushed out. The Cyclops woke with a hideous scream and we immediately scattered out of his reach. He wrenched the stake from his eye and hurled it against the wall. In the dim light of the cave I could see at once that his eyeball was burned right out. The Cyclops would never see again. The cave echoed to his roars of pain and anger and his flocks cowered in their pens as he crashed blindly about, searching for us. Terrified, like the animals, we huddled together amongst them until he gave up the search. Then he called out to his fellow Cyclops across the island. They came rushing to his cave.

"Polyphemus," they shouted, when they had gathered round the entrance, "what on earth is the matter? Has someone attacked you or stolen your flocks that you wake the whole island at this time of night?"

"Noman has attacked me," the Cyclops shouted back. "Noman is hiding in my cave."

"If no one's there then you must be having nightmares," replied the other Cyclops, impatiently. "Go back to bed and let us get some sleep."

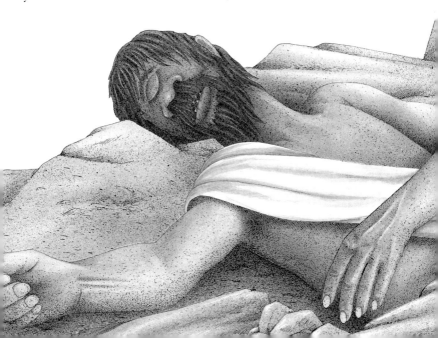

With that they went away, leaving the blinded monster to groan alone. When his friends had gone he groped his way to the entrance and rolled the huge boulder aside. Then he sat in the opening and stretched out his hands on either side, hoping to catch us when we sneaked out.

He should have realized by now that he was not dealing with fools. I chose the biggest rams with the thickest fleeces and fastened them together, three by three. Then we waited.

We waited until dawn. As soon as it was light the rams crowded up to the entrance and began running out to pasture, while the ewes, with their full udders, clamoured to be milked. In his anguish the Cyclops ignored the bleating ewes. He sat in the entrance, feeling the backs of the rams as they squeezed past him. He never thought to feel under their bellies. Once my six companions were through, I clung to the underside of my own ram and took my chance.

Polyphemus stopped my ram at the entrance and plunged his hands into its thick black fleece. My heart was pumping so loudly that I thought the giant was bound to discover me. But he only stroked the ram and sighed and then, with a final groan, he let it run free.

I soon caught up with my companions and untied them. Without wasting a moment, we rounded up dozens of plump sheep and drove them to our waiting ship. My men began to lament their lost comrades but I coldly told them to save their tears for later; I was anxious to sail away from the land of the Cyclops as quickly as we could.

Once we were well clear of the shore I called out to the monster, determined to torment him. "Polyphemus, your cruel hospitality has been rewarded. Perhaps now you'll learn to respect both gods and men."

The Cyclops, who was stumbling blindly about the hillside, turned angrily to the sea when he heard my voice. He tore an enormous rock from the top of the cliffs and hurled it towards us. It narrowly missed our prow and threw up a great wave, washing our ship back towards the beach. I pushed us out of the shallows with a long pole, while my men rowed furiously to carry us out of the monster's rage. When we were twice as far from the shore as before I turned back to face the Cyclops.

My men tried to dissuade me, but I was still bitterly angry and I cried out again. "Polyphemus, last night you asked me my name and I told you it was Noman. You were stupid enough to believe me. Now I want you to know that it wasn't Noman who blinded you but Odysseus, son of Laertes, the destroyer of Troy."

The Cyclops buried his head in his hands and shook it slowly from side to side. "Now I understand," he groaned. "This was all foretold many years ago. But I never suspected that Odysseus would turn out to be a puny little wretch like you. I should have killed you when I had the chance. Now I must pray to my father, Lord Poseidon, god of the sea, to heal my injured eye."

I laughed at the stricken giant. "Your prayers will go unanswered, Polyphemus. Not even Zeus himself could restore your sight. You're blind for life."

"A curse on you, little Greek, and on all your companions!" roared the Cyclops, shaking with rage. "Hear me, my father, Poseidon the earth shaker, and grant your son his heartfelt prayer. May Odysseus never see his home again; however, if he's fated to return, make sure that his journey's long and miserable, that all his companions die and that his is a bitter homecoming."

Poseidon heard his prayer and the curse of the Cyclops has pursued me ever since.

When he had cursed us the monster hurled

another huge rock towards us, but now we were out of range and it fell harmlessly behind us. The wave carried us away from the shore and out of danger. Polyphemus and his fellow Cyclops could not follow us because they had no ships. We had been safe on the smaller island after all.

We soon reached the beach where we had left the main fleet two days before. There we mourned our dead companions and I slaughtered the largest ram to make a special offering to Zeus. It turned out to be a wasted sacrifice.

Afterwards we made a great feast of the sheep that we had stolen from the Cyclops and drank to the memory of our lost comrades. That night we slept where we lay on the beach and when dawn came we put out to sea once more.

CIRCE

We sailed in silence over the desolate sea. It seemed that our journey had been doomed from the start and now great Poseidon himself was against us. We had every reason to be subdued.

After two days we came to an extraordinary floating island, surrounded by a bronze wall, encasing tall cliffs which rose up sheer above it. We moored our ships in the harbour and, with some trepidation after our previous encounters, climbed the stone steps which led up to the city.

We need not have worried. The island belonged to Aeolus, a favourite of the gods, chosen by Zeus to be guardian of the four winds. He treated us to a splendid feast and, when I had told him the story of Troy and of our chequered journey home, he presented me with the perfect gift. It was a bag of strong-hide, tied with a silver cord, which contained three of the four winds. Only the west wind was left free and the west wind would blow us home. When we were safely on the shores of Ithaca I was to release the other winds, but – and Aeolus stressed how important this was – not a moment before.

I blame myself for the disaster which overtook us. For nine days and nights the west wind blew us towards Ithaca. On the morning of the tenth day we could see our own countrymen tending their flocks on the hills and the smoke of a hundred fires curling over the island. Sure that our voyage was at an end, I relaxed into a deep sleep. I had been at the rudder for nine days and nights without once closing my eyes, determined that nothing should go wrong. If only my vigilance had lasted a little longer.

As soon as I was asleep my men began to talk among themselves. I suppose they were carried away by the sight of Ithaca, drunk with the anticipation of the joys of coming home. Greedy, pig-headed fools. They were never to know those joys. They decided to empty the bag Aeolus had given me and share out the contents equally between them.

They got equal shares all right. We all did. Once the winds were loose they blew up a tempest which drove us away from the Ithacan shore. I woke to find us lost on the open sea. My men were weeping over their folly. As for myself, I felt like hurling myself into the raging sea to end it all then and there.

Within three days the winds had driven us back to Aeolus' floating island. I explained what had happened and begged him to help us again. But now Aeolus would have nothing to do with us.

"Get out of here at once, unluckiest of men. Your story shows that the gods are against you, and the godforsaken are not welcome here."

We returned to our ships with his cold words ringing in our ears, and, sick at heart, we sailed away from the island. The winds were unpredictable and the swollen sea made it difficult to row. We were lost yet again and now there was no west wind to blow us home.

For six days and six nights we struggled miserably on, and on the seventh morning we were once more in sight of land. We sailed along the coast until we came to a city with a well-protected harbour overlooked by tall cliffs. I watched the rest of the fleet pass through the narrow harbour entrance and drop their anchors in the still, sheltered waters. Then I ordered my own crew to pull in to the rocks just outside the harbour, where I could conveniently put men ashore to spy out the land.

I sent three men to find out what they could. It was not long before two of them came running back to the ship with a terrible tale to tell. On the road to the town they had met a young woman who told them that the land was called Laestrygonia and that her father, Antiphates, was the king. She pointed out his palace, where they went, in all innocence, to ask for shelter and provisions. Once inside the palace they realized that they had made a dreadful mistake. The Laestrygonians were giants, like the Cyclops, and equally savage. Antiphates seized one of my men and tore him apart. The other two, my trusted cousin Eurylochus and his friend Polites, only just managed to escape.

As they finished their story, hundreds of giant Laestrygonians appeared on the cliff overlooking the harbour and began to hurl huge rocks down onto the ships below. My men struggled desperately to haul in the anchors and get their ships under way, but they were too late. The entire fleet was smashed apart by the bombardment and the survivors were speared like fish and cooked alive on spits by the cruel giants.

Because my own ship was moored outside the

harbour, we were able to slip away unnoticed and unharmed. But our escape was a joyless affair. We brooded over the loss of so many fine comrades and shuddered at the memory of the unspeakable sight we had seen.

After two more wretched days at sea we reached land once again and found a small natural harbour, where we moored our ship and disembarked. Then we simply lay on the beach for two days and nights, overcome with sorrow and exhaustion.

At dawn on the third day, while my men still slept, I took my sword and my spear and ventured out of the camp. I made my way through dense forest until I came to a tall crag. I scrambled to the top and was able to see for miles in every direction.

We had come to a beautiful island, covered in forests and hills, with a wide central plain. A turquoise river meandered across the plain, and as my eyes followed its sinuous path, I saw wisps of smoke floating up from a distant cluster of buildings which I took to be a small village.

My first instinct was to go and investigate but some sixth sense held me back. I decided to return to camp, tell my men what I had seen and lead an expedition across the plain. But my first task would be to organize a hunting party; in our despair, we had not eaten for days.

Not far from our camp I came face to face with a majestic stag making its way down towards the river. In the dense forest it was instantly cornered and, sensing that there was no time to escape, it lowered its great antlers and rushed straight at me. I was ready with my spear, which I drove through the animal's heart. I managed to drag the carcass back to the camp and soon we were enjoying a delicious feast of roast venison washed down with fragrant wine from the hold of our ship.

Now we began to joke and laugh for the first time in days and I told my men what I had seen from my vantage point on the crag. Their faces fell when I told them my plan. After what we had been through their reluctance was understandable, but what was the alternative? We had no idea where we were, no idea which direction to take when we left the island and no provisions apart from wine.

Of the 720 men under my command when we left Troy only forty-five remained. We split into two equal groups and drew lots to see who would explore the island. It fell to my group to stay at the camp. At dawn the following day the others, led by Eurylochus, my trusted cousin, set off through the trees with heavy hearts.

We waited anxiously all day until evening, when Eurylochus came bursting out of the trees and collapsed at our feet. He was pale, trembling and breathless, and when at last he found his voice, his story filled us with gloom.

"Odysseus, my lord, we went as you told us, through the forest and onto the plain. We made our way across it until we came to a magnificent palace. Outside the palace, lions and mountain wolves roamed freely. To our amazement, instead of attacking us or running away, they approached us and fawned over us, as though they expected something from us. They were obviously drugged or enchanted and the look in their eyes was strangely human and inexpressibly sad. As we stood and stared at them, we heard a beautiful song coming from the palace. It was a woman's voice and it sounded so lovely that I knew at once

that it belonged to a goddess. We listened in wonder until the singing
stopped. Then Polites called out and
soon the shining doors of the palace
opened. There stood the goddess. She
smiled at us enticingly and invited us
in. Without a moment's hesitation my
companions entered.

"I alone remained outside. I don't
know why exactly, but she made me
uneasy. There were the lions and
wolves too. There was something
about that look in their eyes that I
couldn't get out of my mind.

"I sat on the ground with my back
against a tree and considered what
to do. I didn't have many choices.
Rather than simply sit and wait or
come back to the camp alone, I decided to find out what was going on in
the palace. I crept round the walls
under cover of the trees until I saw
a magnificent balcony over looking
the river with steps leading up to
it. I hurried up the steps, praying
that wouldn't be seen, and peered

through the great windows which gave out onto the balcony.

"I found myself looking into the main hall of the palace, where I could see my comrades with the goddess and her maids. At first everything appeared to be normal. They were laughing and talking as they ate and drank and I began to think that I'd been an idiot not to go in with them. Before long, however, their eyes glazed over and they slumped drunkenly in their seats. The goddess then pulled out a wand and touched each of them in turn. They ran around on all fours, grunting like pigs. Their faces began to sprout snouts and bristles. Together with her maids, the goddess drove them out to her sties beyond the palace wall.

"When she returned I crept down to the sties to see what had happened. I found, to my horror, that our comrades had indeed been turned into swine. Only their eyes remained human and when I saw their desperate, pleading look, I realized what it was about the lions and wolves which had so troubled me. However, there was nothing I could do to help them and I was terrified of being caught myself. I managed to slip away unnoticed and ran straight back here."

When Eurylochus had finished, my men began to weep and groan for their lost comrades. For my own part, despair had turned to anger while I listened to the story. I was in no mood for tears. I leapt to my feet, grabbed my sword, and asked Eurylochus to lead me to the palace. He fell to his knees and begged me not to go. He was clearly too terrified to help, so I left the camp alone.

I made my way through the forest and across the plain. As I approached the palace a beautiful young man appeared as if from nowhere. His golden sandals and golden wand told me that it was Hermes, son of great Zeus and Maia, the messenger of the gods.

"Unluckiest of men," he said seizing hold of my hand. "I've come to help you for, without my help, the enchantress Circe will turn you into a pig like the rest of your men, to wallow in her sties until you die."

The god bent down and pulled a plant out of the ground. Its flower was milk-white and its root was black as night. "This is moly,"

Hermes said, holding the plant out to me. "Moly is a magic herb which will protect you from Circe's drugs and spells. When she strikes you with her wand, you must draw your sword and threaten to kill her. She will ask you to forgive her and offer to make love to you. This you must accept, for no mortal should refuse the bed of a goddess. However, first make her swear the divine oath that she will do you no harm and that she will release your men. Otherwise she will have you at mercy."

Hermes then flew up into the sky and disappeared as suddenly as he had come. Encouraged by his words and by his magic gift, I walked past the enchanted wolves and lions to the shining doors of Circe's palace. A lovely song came from within but I shut my ears to it and beat loudly on the doors.

Soon they opened and Circe appeared. She was even lovelier than I had imagined. "Noble stranger," she said, in a voice of night and honey, "you are welcome to Circe's house."

Then she took me by the hand and led me into the great hall. I looked around nervously, sensing the danger I was in. The hall was full of beautiful cloth, which Circe had woven, in patterns as intricate and delicate as spiders' webs. As the goddess mixed my wine with her stupefying potions, I had the unpleasant sensation of being a juicy fly which she had enticed into her web.

"Noble stranger, please try this," said Circe softly, handing me a golden cup. "I think you'll like it." She smiled as I drank it, trusting the moly to protect me.

Immediately Circe was upon me with her wand. "There, stupid man, become the pig you really are. I'll drive you to my sties where you can root around in the dirt with the others."

I drew my sword before she had finished speaking. Now I held it to her throat. Circe shrieked, fell to the ground and clasped her arms around my knees. "Noble stranger, forgive me. I thought you were another wretched man come begging at my doorstep. Now I see that I was wrong to despise you." She lifted her head and gazed imploringly into my eyes. "No man has ever resisted my drugs and spell before. You must be Odysseus himself for Hermes has always warned me that you would come. Now that you're here, let me welcome you as a great hero deserves. Put away your bright sword and come to my bed, where I'll make you forget your sorrow and your suffering."

"Lovely Circe," I replied coldly, without lowering my sword, "how can you expect me to trust you? First you try to drug me and cast your vile spells; now you offer to love me. Meanwhile my dear companions grunt helplessly in your sties. Only the gods know how many miserable souls wander this island, trapped in the alien bodies of lions and wolves. Once you have me in your bed, naked and without my sword, what's to stop you from bewitching me too? No, first you must swear a divine oath to free my men and do nothing more to harm us."

Circe swore the oath then led me out to the sties and told me to fling open the doors. As the swine came running out, one by one, she touched them with her wand. At once they changed back into the shape of my comrades. They looked lost and shaken but they were younger and more handsome than I remembered. It took them a few moments to recover, but when they saw me standing next to Circe they were overjoyed and wept as I embraced them. Even Circe was affected.

She interrupted us, saying: "Noble Odysseus, son of Laertes, why don't you go back to your camp and fetch the rest of your men? If you stow your ship and your belongings in the caves above the beach they'll be perfectly safe. Then bring your men back to my palace. I and my maids will bathe you and entertain you and serve you delicious wine and sumptuous food. I hope that you'll then be able to forgive me and that we can be friends. You won't regret it, I promise you."

Bad luck and disappointment had haunted us since we left Troy. Most of our companions had died hideous, violent deaths. The suffering and hardship we had endured now made the temptations of Circe's palace irresistible. Leaving the men I had rescued in the tender hands of Circe's maids, I went back to the camp. I was only just in time. Our comrades had given us all up and were preparing to sail.

As soon as they saw me they rushed up to me and overwhelmed me with questions and

embraces. They could hardly have been more excited if we had finally landed in Ithaca. When I had calmed them down and explained the situation, only Eurylochus was reluctant to come with me.

He shouted to win our attention. "It's madness to think of going back. We'll all be at that cruel witch's mercy. What makes you think she'll keep her promise? She'll just laugh at us and turn us back into pigs."

"Eurylochus," I replied, "if you want to stay here on your own, then stay. But the rest of us are going to Circe's palace to enjoy ourselves and forget our sorrows." Then, afraid that I had been too hard on him, I put my arms round his shoulders and spoke more gently. "Come, dear cousin, think of what you went through as a bad dream. It's over now, believe me. Circe has sworn a divine oath not to harm us. If she breaks it Zeus will punish her."

Reluctantly, Eurylochus agreed to come. The rest of my men were in a hurry to rejoin their lost comrades and we soon reached the palace. We were delighted to be back together and our happy cries echoed through the great hall. Even Eurylochus became himself again when he realized that his nightmare was over.

For Circe was as good as her word. We were all bathed in scented baths and wrapped in dazzling clothes she herself had made. Then a magnificent feast was set before us and wine of a fragrance that would have delighted the gods. Later Circe took me by the hand and led me to her bed. My men were left to enjoy the company of her maids.

Enchanted by pleasure, we stayed in Circe's palace for a year. I had quite forgotten my home and my wife until one day my men came up to me and told me it was time to leave. I knew at once that they were right. When I told her, Circe became sad and I thought, for a moment, that she would try to prevent us. But she was resigned to our decision.

"If you're determined to leave now then so be it. I'm afraid that your way home won't be easy. Poseidon still seeks to destroy you. What's more, his brother Zeus has decreed that you must descend to the underworld and visit the spirits of the dead before you can return home."

"But, sweet Circe," I replied, dismayed, "how can I possibly go to the grim house of Hades? No one has ever been and returned to tell the tale."

"It will find you," said Circe, as she clasped my trembling hand. "Raise your mast, set your sail and the north wind will take you there. At the entrance to the underworld you must sacrifice a ram and a black ewe, which I will give you. Their blood will call up the spirits of the dead. Burn the sheep and pray to Hades and Persephone, the gods of the underworld. Then the spirits will talk to you. When your visit is over, come back here to refresh yourselves before your journey home."

We sat in silence and waited for the dawn. There was nothing left to say or do. At first light I led my men down to the beach. We dragged our ship to the water and checked the timbers and the rigging. Then we loaded our treasures into the hold and put out to sea in dread. For who could set sail for the land of the dead and not be sick at heart?

ODYSSEUS AND THE GHOSTS

The north wind blew, as Circe had foretold, and sped us on our way towards the land of perpetual night. The sun was low in the sky by the time we reached the mouth of the river Ocean and it set behind us as we sailed up river. I have no idea how long it took us; all sense of time had disappeared, but eventually the river dwindled to a stream and we hauled our ship out of the water onto a narrow strip of beach. Peering through the gloom, we could make out the groves of blighted willow and tall black poplars which belong to Persephone, daughter of Zeus and queen of death. We took the two sheep, and made our way through the groves, beside the tiny stream that the river Ocean had become, until we reached its source at the very entrance to the underworld.

Here we stopped and my men dug a trench like a grave while I prayed for the multitude of my dead comrades. Then,

while my companions held the ram and the black ewe over the trench, I took out my knife and slit the animals' throats. Their blood gushed out , first in great spurts then in a steady stream which poured into the grave-like hole. At once the spirits of the dead appeared at the entrance to the underworld and crowded, jostling and screeching, towards the trench, drawn by the scent of blood. I pulled out my bright sword and rushed towards them, waving it about my head. Although I could not harm them, for how can you hurt a ghost, they were clearly dismayed by the sight of me and drew back in terror. Then, while I held off the unquiet spirits of the night, my companions skinned the dead sheep and burnt them, praying over the smoke and flames to Hades and Persephone.

While my men prayed, I sat with my sword held out over the blood-filled trench. Now the spirits grew still and approached me one by one. The first to come forward was my mother, Anticleia. When I saw her the blood drained from my face and my heart stopped. Twelve years before I had left her happy and well, in the full bloom of middle age, and now she was dead. I felt a sharp pang of fear. What about Penelope, my wife, and Telemachus, my son? Were they dead too? Had some disaster struck my home? I longed to embrace my mother and question her, but to my dismay she looked straight through me without a flicker of recognition. I waved her away, in spite of my tears, and watched her melt back into the shapeless mass of dead souls.

As my mother withdrew another ghost approached. It was a blind old man with a golden staff, who stopped in front of me. "Cunning Odysseus, famous sacker of cities," he began, in a hoarse whisper that pierced the surrounding silence, "I see your bad luck has finally brought you to this land of sorrow and of night. I am Teiresias, the Theban prophet. Because of my wisdom in life, Persephone has made me spokesman for the wretched souls of the dead. Stand back from the trench and let me taste the fresh blood of your sacrifice, then I'll tell you what to expect on your journey home."

I drew back, as he asked, and the blind ghost knelt down and lowered his face until his lips reached the pool of dark blood. It was a horrifying sight and, when he raised his head, the wet blood glistened on his shadowy lips.

"Unluckiest of men," began Teiresias, "you are desperate to return home, yet the god of the sea is determined to prevent you. He wants revenge for his son, Polyphemus, and he's sworn not to give up until you're either dead or safely home in Ithaca. You may eventually get there but your journey will be perilous. Above all, avoid the island of Thrinacia, where the sun-god Hyperion's sheep and cattle graze. If any of your men lays a finger on these animals then your ship and your crew will be destroyed by Zeus. As for you, if you reach home at all it will be many years later and you will find many unwelcome guests in your house. Only if you overcome these pretenders to your bed and throne can you look forward to a long life and a happy old age. And remember, beware Poseidon. He has a long memory.'

"Wise Teiresias," I replied, "I shall keep your warning close to my heart. But now, please tell me, how can I speak to these other ghosts? There are so many things that I want to ask them."

"All you have to do," he answered, "is to let them drink as I drank, from the blood of your sacrifice."

Teiresias disappeared into the crowd of ghosts. Now my mother, Anticleia, came forward once more and I let her drink her fill of the blood. When she raised her head from the dark pool she recognized me at once.

"Odysseus, my dearest child, what has brought you to this place of death and sorrow? Are you still wandering the seas, far from home?"

I tried to hug her to me as she spoke, but my hands went straight through her ghostly outline. Tears rolled down my cheeks as I replied. "Dearest mother, it seems that I'm destined to wander the seas forever, far from my home and loved ones. The story of my suffering is already too long to tell you. But what of you? How did you die? How is my family? Has something terrible happened to them too?"

"No, no, they're still alive," said my mother, smiling sadly to think of them. "Your father, Laertes, now lives alone on his mountain farm, grieving for you. As for Penelope, she's remained loyal all these years and still longs for you. But it's difficult for her. There's pressure on her to take another husband in your place; the people say that they need a king. Otherwise she manages things well enough and Telemachus will soon be old enough to help her. He's already a fine young man, a son you can be proud of."

My mother paused while we both thought of our family in Ithaca and cried, softly, for our lost happiness. Then, still sobbing, my mother spoke through her ghostly tears. "Like your dear father, I was overcome with grief when you didn't return from Troy. Unlike him, I was too frail to endure the disappointment and I died pining for you, my dearest son. You were my pride and joy, Odysseus, and I couldn't bear this life without you."

Again I tried to embrace her and again she disappeared within my arms. Then she was gone and Persephone, queen of death, sent forward another shadowy figure in her place. I was shocked to see the sorrowful face of Agamemnon, supreme commander of our Greek forces at Troy, son of Atreus and brother of Menelaus.

When he had drunk the dark blood, he slowly lifted his head. "Odysseus, dear friend, what brings you alive to the grim house of death?"

"Great Agamemnon," I replied, "the gods

have sent me to this dreadful place to meet the spirits of the dead. But I never expected to find you here. To think that, after all those years of war, you were destined not to reach your home."

"Oh, I got home all right," groaned Agamemnon, "and I wish I never had. It was no longer my home. We had a following wind all the way from 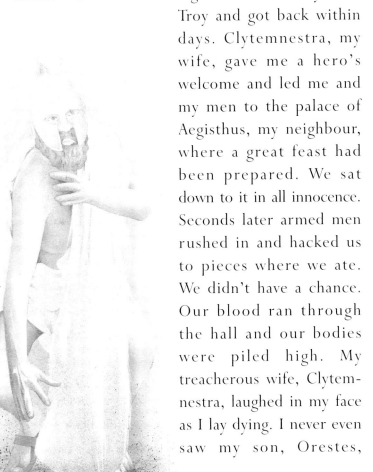 Troy and got back within days. Clytemnestra, my wife, gave me a hero's welcome and led me and my men to the palace of Aegisthus, my neighbour, where a great feast had been prepared. We sat down to it in all innocence. Seconds later armed men rushed in and hacked us to pieces where we ate. We didn't have a chance. Our blood ran through the hall and our bodies were piled high. My treacherous wife, Clytemnestra, laughed in my face as I lay dying. I never even saw my son, Orestes, before she killed me. And now the two murderers share my throne."

When Agamemnon had finished, his unhappy spirit withdrew, weeping, and another dead soul stepped out of the shadows to drink the dark blood. It was Achilles, the finest of our warriors at Troy. He still had the air of a great prince, even as a ghost. But when I told him so he laughed at me sadly.

"Noble Odysseus, you of all men should know better than to be deceived by appearances. To be great among the dead is to be nothing. In Hades all men are equal. I'd rather be the poorest man alive than walk among these lonely spirits here. But let's not talk of death. Have you any news of my beloved son Neoptolemus, who was barely a man when I died on the dusty plains of Troy?"

"Indeed I do," I replied, glad to be the messenger of good news for a change. "After your death I went myself to fetch him from the island of Scyros. He proved wise beyond his years and brave in battle and carried away rich treasure from Troy's smoking ruins."

Achilles thanked me from his heart and faded from my presence, smiling happily at the thought of his son.

Now other spirits approached me and drank

the blood. Some I knew, others were unfamiliar, faces from the distant past. Then Persephone herself appeared and led me through the crowded entrance into the underworld itself.

The touch of her cold hand chilled my blood as we walked down deep into the cavern of endless emptiness. I saw Tityus and Tantalus, Sisyphus and Heracles and many more besides, condemned to suffer torment until the end of time. It was not long before the sight of souls in agony and the din of hideous screams became unbearable. I begged Persephone to let me go, terrified that she would keep me alive in this hell. Somehow I found myself back outside. Now I was completely alone. There were no ghosts and my companions, too, had disappeared.

I ran back past the tall black poplars and through the groves of blighted willows. My heart was pounding and my mind was numb with fear. Perhaps my men had already sailed away from the shores of Hades, thinking that I was lost to the world of the living. I would be left to wander alone in the half-light of this miserable place until my death.

But the ship was still there. My men had waited. I waded through the freezing, black water of Ocean and a dozen arms reached down to haul me over the side of the boat. They immediately set the sail and pulled in the anchor. With the wind behind us and my men rowing furiously, the shores of Hades were already fading in the distance by the time I had recovered my breath.

SCYLLA AND CHARYBDIS

We rowed on down river, helped by the wind. We could barely make out the murky outlines of the river bank and the only sound was the regular splash of the oars. On and on we rowed through the dank gloom. It seemed like an age before we pulled out of Ocean into the open sea.

The Mediterranean night came as a relief after the everlasting night of Hades. The full moon threw a pool of soft golden light across the water and a thousand bright stars studded the sky. Now, at last, we could relax and my men rested their oars, and lay back exhausted.

I sat at the helm while my men slept. A steady southerly filled the sails and blew us on our way. With only the moon and stars for company, my mind turned back to the unhappy spirits of the dead. I wept for the souls of my lost comrades and, above all, for my dear mother. Towards morning, when my tears ran dry, my thoughts moved on to the voyage to come. It was a weary prospect. After all we had been through, we were still as far away as ever from Ithaca, our home.

We sailed on through that night and most of the following day. It was early evening by the time we reached Aeaea, and Circe and her maids were looking out for us on the beach. They had brought us food, which we devoured greedily, and fragrant wine to wash it down. Afterwards Circe took my hand and led me down the beach.

"I want to talk with you alone," she said, "for you must leave at dawn and there are many things you need to know."

We walked to the edge of the pine forest above the beach and sat down in the shade of the trees. I breathed in the deep, heady scent of pine resin and rested my eyes on Circe's lovely face. She hesitated before she spoke and I sensed that she wanted to ask me to stay. In all truth I cannot swear that I would have refused.

But the moment passed. When the goddess spoke it was not of love but of dangers yet to come. Teiresias, it seemed, had only told me half the story. Circe's soft words told me the rest.

"Dear Odysseus," she began, "unlucky man, the jealous gods will give you no peace. You have returned unscathed from grim Hades' house only to face still greater trials. Listen carefully and promise to do exactly as I say." The goddess took my hand in hers and made me swear this solemnly, by the great gods and everything dear to me.

Then she went on: "Dear Odysseus, your voyage home will be more perilous than any battle on the dusty plains of Troy. Vengeful Poseidon is determined to destroy you and the other gods will do nothing to stop him. Since Zeus has forbidden it, even Athene cannot help you. Once you leave these shores you are on your own.

"From Aeaea you must steer due south; the north wind will carry you along. Towards evening you will come to the island of the Sirens, three cruel enchantresses whose sweet song is irresistible to men. They will implore you to come ashore, but once ashore you are lost. Their heavenly song will turn to hideous shrieks as they tear your flesh apart. I shall give you special wax to block up your ears, for if you are deaf to their music you will be safe.

"Once past the Sirens, you will sail on undisturbed until you approach the straits which divide the northern part of Thrinacia, where Hyperion keeps his golden cattle, from the mainland. Here you will have to make a choice. If you avoid the straits and sail round the west coast of Thrinacia, you will come to the Wanderers, a field of huge rocks scattered across the water. From a distance few sights could look more inviting. Glistening in the sun, the deep blue rocks appear to float on the surface of the turquoise sea. The water is deep and mirror-smooth and there is room between the rocks for easy navigation.

"Close to, however, the picture changes. Once a ship comes within range, the rocks turn grey and craggy. An icy wind whistles among them over the turbulent sea and black clouds mass overhead. The rocks themselves begin to move, slowly at first, heaving and swaying from side to side, while deep groans like distant thunder drag themselves up from the bottom of the sea. Then the rocks move faster and faster until they hurtle about and crash together. Any ship would be smashed apart in that chaos; it would be suicide to go that way.

"So you must enter the straits, where you will pass between two fateful cliffs. One of them towers into the sky; the other is about half its size. An enormous fig-tree grows straight out from the smaller cliff. It's a curious sight, but don't be tempted to look closer. An awesome monster, Charybdis, wallows on the sea-bed there. Three times a day she stretches her vast tentacles out and swirls the water round, then sucks it greedily down, devouring whatever the whirlpool brings her.

"Half-way up the taller cliff you'll see the entrance to a cave. Deep in its foul recesses lives the hideous sea-hag, Scylla. Scylla has twelve legs and six monstrous heads. She sits in her own filth, whining and yelping like a little puppy, waiting for her prey. She will certainly seize a man with each of her gruesome heads as you pass by. Nevertheless, I urge you to go that way. Far better to lose six men than to risk losing your ship and all your lives.

"Finally, remember what Teiresias told you and avoid Thrinacia altogether. If you are forced to put ashore there then, whatever you do, be sure to leave Hyperion's sheep and cattle alone. Otherwise you will lose your ship, your men and perhaps even your life."

Circe squeezed my hand for the last time. Tears glistened on her cheeks as she turned away from me and, without another word, hurried off through the trees.

The sky was already reddening in the east and my men were stirring on the beach. We loaded the stores which Circe had given us and put out to sea once more. As the goddess had foretold there was a north wind to carry us along and soon we had left the island of Aeaea far behind. Now I repeated Circe's sombre warnings to my men, although I did not tell them about the Scylla. If there was nothing we could do to avoid her, then it would only have caused unnecessary alarm.

We sailed on through the day and towards evening the island of the Sirens loomed over the horizon. I took the ball of soft wax, which Circe had given me, from its leather pouch and set about plugging my crew's ears. When I had finished I shouted to test my work. Not one of them heard me. Then I got my men to lash me to the mast and waited, nervously, as we approached the island. We were still a long way off when the first strains of the Sirens' heavenly song drifted enticingly across the water.

"Noble Odysseus," they sang, "greatest of the Greeks, destroyer of Troy, come stay with us and listen to our song. No one who hears it can resist our music; the memory of it will stay with you to the end of your days. Come ashore, Odysseus, and we will sing as we have never sung before."

I was instantly seduced by the sweet sound of their voices, drunk on the nectar of their song. If strong ropes had not held me, then Circe's warning words would have counted for nothing. I was desperate to go ashore but my men were deaf to my frenzied screams. They gazed, unmoved, at the furious contortions of my face and rowed steadily on.

By now we had sailed close in to the island, where the three Sirens sat on a cliff top and watched us approach. They were as beautiful as their voices which, when we drew closer, became unbearably lovely. I struggled to escape until the ropes bit into my flesh, convinced now that Circe had tricked me. She had not been worried about my safety at all; it was jealousy that made her want to keep me from the Sirens. But it was not long before I was brought to my senses with a jolt.

The cliff on which the Sirens sat formed part of a narrow headland which we now began to skirt. As soon as the Sirens realized that we were not putting ashore, a hideous change came over them. The beautiful young women turned into terrifying hags, half-woman and half-vulture, and instead of their sweet song a stream of ugly shrieks and curses filled the air.

Once we had rounded the headland the horrible sound faded away behind us and my men untied me and unblocked their ears. They asked me to describe the music which had so bewitched me, but before I had time to reply we were all silenced by the grim sight which now met our eyes.

We were sailing down the east side of the headland, past a small, sandy beach backed by huge cliffs. A line of jagged rocks lurked menacingly just beneath the surface of the sea and the beach was piled high with whitened bones. At the top of the pile lay the Sirens' most recent victims, covered in dark stains. The thousands of skeletons beneath them had been bleached by the sun and the salt sea. We were sickened by the sight of what might have been our fate and thankful to leave that gruesome place behind.

Now we made good progress. The wind was still with us, the twilight sky was clear and the sea calm. We sailed on through the night taking it in turns to keep watch and steer. Refreshed by sleep and encouraged by our swift progress, my crew were in a hopeful mood when morning came. It did not last long.

The sun was still rising when we saw the straits ahead of us in the distance. We could see the Wanderers away to our right, just as Circe had described them, glistening in the sun. We entered the straits and before long the fateful cliffs of Scylla and Charybdis came into view. The two cliffs stood opposite each other at the narrowest point of the straits. At first they looked harmless enough, but, closer to, a large area of water in front of the smaller cliff appeared to be simmering. Soon the water began to steam and churn around, until a huge whirlpool formed where Charybdis sucked the water down. My men froze in terror as our ship was drawn to the edge.

"For the gods' sake row, before it's too late!" I screamed, only just in time. The ship was slowly beginning to turn before we pulled clear.

We had escaped from Charybdis, but only into the shadow of the larger cliff. I could see the entrance half-way up the rock but no sound came from the cave. Perhaps the Scylla was asleep and we would get away unscathed. Suddenly there was a thunderous boom across the water. We turned to see a towering fountain thrown up as Charybdis blew the whirlpool out.

While our backs were turned and the spray from the fountain fell on our cheeks, ghastly yelping broke out in our midst. The Scylla's six heads, all fangs, foul breath and matted hair, were amongst us and seized six of the crew. They wriggled

helplessly in her ugly mouths as she drew in her scaly necks. Then she devoured them alive on the ledge outside her cave, yelping and whining hideously all the while. There was nothing we could do and, sick at heart, we rowed away from the cliffs.

Now I was determined to sail on until we had left these straits of death far behind. I thought we would be sure then of a safe passage home. I little realized that our greatest trial was still to come.

CALYPSO'S PRISONER

We sailed out of the straits, with the hideous yelping of the Scylla still ringing in our ears, and turned our ship eastwards, towards home. We intended to skirt the southern tip of the mainland and wait for a fair wind to carry us across the Adriatic Sea. We were prepared to wait for as long as proved necessary; we wanted to be absolutely sure that nothing went wrong now.

Sadly for us, the gods had other ideas. As soon as we swung out into the open sea, fierce easterly winds and currents drove us back towards Thrinacia. We hauled in the sails and I urged my comrades to row for their lives, but they were no match for the elements. As the afternoon wore on their heads began to droop and the tempo of their oar-strokes slowly dropped. Still the elements drove us back and still I urged my men on, in desperation now. They were exhausted. It was Eurylochus who finally spoke out for them and demanded to turn back.

Reluctantly I agreed. With a heavy

heart, I ordered my crew to turn the boat around. We pulled up the sails and now the wind swept us towards the Thrinacian coast. My men joked that, once again, we were sailing in the wrong direction, but I did not share their laughter. I sat apart, in the stern, and stared at our wake. It was quickly lost in the choppy water and this, for some reason, added to my sense of impending doom.

By the time we reached the island the sun had already sunk behind the mountains and the light was fading fast. We sailed straight into the beautiful cove, sheltered by tall cliffs. My comrades leapt into the shallows and dragged our boat up onto the sand. The sound of bleating and lowing had carried to us across the water and now, in the twilight, we could make out the shapes of sheep and cattle moving about on the hillside. On the ridge their silhouettes stood out against the sky.

My men began to lick their lips. It had been a long gruelling day and they looked forward to a feast. Straightway I jumped up onto the boat which lay beside us, and pulled out my sword to back up my words.

"My friends, listen to me now and listen well." I spoke slowly, letting my gaze rest on each of the faces below me. "This is the famous island of Thrinacia, which belongs to Hyperion, god of the sun. Here his sheep and cattle graze, seven herds of fifty cows and seven flocks of fifty sheep. These animals are his pride and joy and, if you touch them, then your next voyage will be your last. Both Teiresias and Circe have foretold it. You must swear a solemn oath to leave these beasts alone."

My men had no wish to anger the gods and quickly swore the oath. Then we took cured hams and cheese, fruit and wine from our ship's shallow hold and made a fire on the beach to keep off the night chill. We ate hungrily after the day's exertions and drank to the souls of our lost comrades. As they drank my men began to weep and, as they wept, sweet sleep overcame them. I, however, remained dry-eyed and alert. I stared into the glowing embers of the fire and prayed for a fair wind to carry us home.

My prayers went unanswered. By dawn a violent storm had blown up and we gazed in dismay at the turbulent sea. The wind reached gale force and huge waves crashed into the rocks at the entrance to our cove, throwing great sheets of spray high over the cliff tops. We would have to wait a few days at least, that much was clear. To begin with we waited patiently enough. We had Circe's supplies to feed us and her fragrant wine to keep up our spirits. The days passed and the storm settled down; now we waited for the wind to change. But the days slowly turned into weeks and the strong south-easterly continued to blow. We watched our supplies steadily dwindle and the worm of anxiety gnawed at our minds.

A month passed and still the south-easterly blew. Now our supplies were finished and it was the worm of hunger that gnawed at our insides. We scoured the rocks for crabs and shellfish and made hooks and lines to fish in the sea, but the little we caught only teased our appetites and made our hunger worse. Then we roamed the wooded hills of Thrinacia in search of game, but there was none to be found. And all around us Hyperion's golden cattle and snow-white sheep grazed peacefully while we starved. Even when we sat on the beach and looked out to sea, away from the hills, the sound of lowing cattle and bleating sheep was always in our ears. My men were at the end of their tether.

As a last resort I left my companions on the beach and walked up into the nearby hills. Weak from hunger and lack of sleep, I struggled on until I reached the highest ridge. From the summit

I had a commanding view of the south-east coast-line and back across the island to the central mountain range. It was a holy place. I knelt down and bared my soul to the gods, while the sun went down over the distant mountains. Then soft sleep crept up behind me and took me unawares.

When I woke the sun was already high in the sky. My long sleep had refreshed me and my hunger seemed miraculously to have disappeared. On my way back down to the beach, I realized that the wind had at long last changed. I thought that our trials were over.

The wind was now blowing down from the hills. I only smelt the roasting flesh when I came to the beach. In spite of my warnings and in breach of their solemn promise, my men had helped themselves to Hyperion's cattle.

"Noble Odysseus," said Eurylochus, who was the first to see me, "don't be dismayed. We know this is forbidden meat, but what choice did we have? We've made proper sacrifices to the gods and promised to build Hyperion a magnificent temple if we're allowed to return home safely."

Too dismayed to be angry I buried my face in my hands. If only I had stayed on the beach. Surely I could have persuaded my companions to wait just one more day. By now we could have left the shores of Thrinacia far behind. Instead my men had broken divine law and could expect no mercy. Hyperion would have his revenge.

There was a sudden gasp from my companions. I looked up to see the carcasses of the slaughtered cattle writhe and shiver where they lay on the sand. At the same time, the meat which my men were already roasting on spits began to bellow like cattle in pain. The gods had spoken and my men were seized with terror. They begged me to leave the island at once.

"Whether we stay or go makes no difference now," I replied, "but since you wish to go then let us go."

Without another word we dragged our ship down to the water, raised the mast and sails and rowed away from the shore. The slaughtered cattle still lay writhing on the sand and the bellows of the roasting meat echoed round the cove as we sailed out into open sea.

Hardly had the sound faded behind us when black clouds massed over head and a sudden tempest whipped up the sea. Clinging to the mast I looked up to see great Zeus himself burst out of the clouds with an arm raised high above his head. In the next instant his arm came down and hurled his dreaded thunderbolt straight at our ship. The vessel exploded and those men not killed by the blast were drowned.

I alone survived. But it seemed that I had only been saved for a more horrible end. I had clung to the mast as the ship broke up around me and it kept me afloat in the seething water. The storm soon abated but our old friend, the south-easterly wind, now returned to drive me back towards the grim straits of Scylla and Charybdis. All through the night that same wind blew and, when morning came, I saw the dreaded cliffs ahead of me. Before I knew it, I was racing towards the small cliff. I was only metres away when the water began to churn. Charybdis was sucking her whirlpool in.

I clung to the mast and shut my eyes. There was nothing I could do. Seconds later the far end was sucked down with such violence that I was cata pulted high up into the branches of the fig-tree that grows out of the cliff.

Now I could see right down to the bottom of the whirlpool, where the hideous monster lay. Her vast tentacles swirled the water round, and her bulbous, octopus eyes stared greedily up, waiting for me to fall. But I held on and waited, for one hour, then another and still she sucked the whirlpool in. Finally, Charybdis could hold it in no longer and with a great gush the undigested contents of her belly flew into the air around me. As soon as the water had settled I dived and swam furiously away from the cliff. The mast was floating in the middle of the straits and I managed to grab hold of it once more. Now I was within reach of the cruel Scylla, but Zeus must have been watching over me; a powerful current carried me out of the straits, before she sensed that I was there.

For nine days and nights I drifted with the currents. They took me round the south-east headland of Thrinacia, but although I was parched and hungry I dared not set foot on those fateful shores again. Then the currents carried me slowly westwards, further and further away from my long-lost home. On the tenth morning I was finally washed up on an unknown shore. I was too weak to move and my throat too dry to utter a sound. I lay on the burning sand, beneath the cruel sun, waiting to die.

Then I must have passed out because Calypso told me later that she had found me lying on the beach, unconscious and half-dead. She dragged me back to her cavern of marble and gold, and nursed me back to life. I opened my eyes to see the lovely nymph staring down at me, her braided hair falling towards my face. She had laid me on a bed of the softest down, covered my burnt, cracked skin with cold wet cloths and poured cool spring-water between my parched lips. I tried to speak, but no words came. She placed a finger over my mouth and smiled her lovely smile. I gazed at her in wonder until I fell into a deep sleep.

I slept long and often over the following weeks as I gradually regained my strength. When I was awake Calypso would sit by my bed while I recounted the story of Troy and told her of my ill-fated journey home. I learnt, in turn, that she was an immortal nymph who lived alone on her island, Ogygia. Her father was Atlas, the Titan who holds up the sky. She had been warned of my arrival, for my fame went before me even among the gods. She said that I should stay with her until I had fully recovered.

Soon it was clear that she wanted me to stay much longer. Calypso had fallen in love with me and offered me the gift of eternal life if I would live with her forever. It is hard to refuse a goddess, but I longed for Ithaca and Penelope, my wife. I pleaded with her to let me go. But she would not give me up. And so my life with Calypso began.

One year passed and then another. Every morning I went down to the beach on the eastern shore of Ogygia and looked out across the sea, pining for my home. Meanwhile, Calypso sat at her loom in her sumptuous cavern in the woods and sang in a voice like Circe's as she wove her beautiful cloth. Every evening, while the sun set behind me on the far side of the island, I made my way wearily back through the cypress woods to the enchanted grove in front of Calypso's cavern. Here vines and wild roses grew in abundance and, hidden among them, nightingales sang. Small grassy meadows, thick with wild flowers, sloped down to clear streams, fed by the crystal waters of the four springs which bubbled up in the grove. It was a heavenly place, fit for a god, and Calypso was more beautiful than any mortal woman. But it was not my home and deep in my heart I was sad.

Seven years passed and still I yearned for Ithaca. Then, one evening, I returned from the beach to find Calypso sobbing on her bed; her face buried in the pillows. I put out a hand to comfort her, but she flinched from my touch. I sat beside the bed and waited. At last, she turned her face towards me, pale and red-eyed.

"Dear, brave Odysseus," she said in a trembling voice, "rejoice. You have your wish at last. Great Zeus has ordered me to let you go and, though it breaks my heart, I must obey him." She took me in her arms and held me close as though she would never let me go.

At dawn Calypso brought me a bronze axe, an adze and a box of finely balanced tools. Then she took me to a place where a stand of silver fir rose tall and straight into the sky. I set to work at once. During the days which followed I felled twenty of the finest trees, cleaned them and cut the timber to size. I shaped the wood and pegged and jointed the pieces together. When I had finished I had a small boat in which to make my journey home. Calypso brought me cloth for the sail and rope for the braces and halyards and I was ready to put to sea.

It was early dawn when Calypso led me down to the beach and helped me load my boat with

water, food and wine. Then I took her hand and asked her to understand my desire to grow old and die with my wife and family around me. Neither the beauty of a goddess nor the promise of immortality could ever mean as much to me. She smiled sadly and shook her head. "I will never understand the ways of men. Go now. May Zeus watch over you, for I wish you well. If you keep the Great Bear to your left, you will steer a true course for home." With these words she turned away from me and disappeared forever through the trees.

RETURN TO ITHACA

I watched her go before I pushed my boat out through the shallows. I had a fair west wind and soon Ogygia had faded in the distance. For seventeen days and nights I kept a constant watch and at dawn on the eighteenth day my beloved Ithaca came into view. Then, while I wept tears of joy, cruel fate caught up with me as it had nine years before. On that occasion my careless men released the winds. Now vengeful Poseidon saw his chance to destroy me.

You know the rest. Somehow I survived and reached these shores. My story is at an end and I pray my wanderings will soon be over too.

Odysseus had finished and silence fell over the hall. His tale had entranced the Phaeacians and now, as his voice died away in the shadows, they remained lost in another world.

King Alcinous finally broke the spell. "Noble Odysseus, your story has touched our hearts and will move all those who hear it until the end of time. I pray that your trials and sorrows are ended, yet who knows what awaits you even now in Ithaca? That lies in the hands of the immortal gods. But this at least I can promise. Tomorrow your long journey will be over and you will tread your native soil again."

Here the king paused and gestured to his wine-bearer, who stepped forward and knelt before him on the marble floor. "Go down to the cellar," said Alcinous. "Bring up that ancient stone jar which stands behind all the others, covered in dust and cobwebs. It holds the last of the fragrant wine which my grandfather, Poseidon, gave to my father, Nausithous, when I was born. We will drink it now to wish Odysseus a safe voyage home."

The wine-bearer fetched the jar and poured out the heady wine. The ceremonial cup was passed from hand to hand around the hall. Finally it reached Odysseus, who rose to his feet and took it in both hands.

"Noble Arete and Alcinous, I wish you and all in your house a long life and an old age full of joy. As for myself, Zeus willing, I look forward to a happier time when I can enjoy your generous gifts and remember your great kindness."

He raised the cup to his lips and drained it in one draught. Then, with a last farewell, he made his way past the long table under the wondering gaze of the Phaeacian lords, and stepped over the bronze threshold, out of the great hall.

Outside the light was fading fast. A full moon, massive and burnished gold, already shone overhead. As Odysseus crossed the palace courtyard, a tall slender figure emerged from the shadows and fell in beside him. It was the princess Nausicaa.

They walked in silence down through the assembly-place to the harbour, where his ship was waiting. The chest full of gifts was already stowed in the hold and the crew sat ready at the oars.

As they stood at the water's edge the princess took Odysseus by the hand. "Dear friend from across the seas," she said softly, "I wish you well, although I fear one further trial remains, as testing as any you've yet endured. I pray you'll overcome it and that you may enjoy a long life in peace and happiness with your lovely wife. I've only one thing to ask of you: that you'll always remember the young princess who found you when you were lost and wretched and helped you in your hour of need. Go now and wish me well, dear friend."

"I swear it," promised Odysseus, returning the gentle pressure of her hand, "by mighty

Zeus and all the gods."

Their hands parted and Odysseus leapt on board. At once the sailors released the mooring and the ship drew smoothly away from the shore. Odysseus stood on the half-deck and looked back at the harbour where a single figure stood motionless, watching him go. Then he turned to the open sea and gazed across the moonlit water. Ahead lay Ithaca. His heart was already there. Soon his deep weariness overcame him and he fell asleep to the swish of the prow cutting through the water and the rhythmical splashing of the oars.

He woke with a start to find that it was daylight and that the rocking of the boat had stopped. He was all alone on a sandy beach and the chest full of gifts lay beside him. His heart sank; it seemed he had been abandoned on some unknown shore. Then, as his eyes took in the surroundings, his heart leapt with joy.

The beach was at the head of a natural harbour, enclosed within tall cliffs. Above the beach the entrance to a cave was partially concealed by an ancient olive tree. Odysseus knew this place well. The cave was sacred to the Naiads, nymphs of the rivers and springs, who sat inside it and wove their purple cloth on the banks of ever-flowing streams. The harbour was sacred to the old sea-god Phorcys, father-in-law of Poseidon. But Odysseus had no fear of Poseidon here, nor would the curse of Polyphemus ever trouble him again. For he was standing on dry land and the sand beneath his feet was the sand of Ithaca, his home.

He fell to his knees and kissed the ground, soaking it with tears. He did not see the goddess Athene appear at his side.

"Dear Odysseus, welcome home at last," said the goddess, smiling down at him. "It is good that you

should ease your heart with tears. But calm yourself now and listen to me carefully. For your troubles are far from over."

Odysseus paled and a thousand anxious thoughts flashed through his mind. "Divine Athene, daughter of great Zeus, please tell me the worst at once. I need to know. Has cruel fate snatched my wife or son before my return or have been betrayed by those I love? Does some stranger wallow in my bed and sit in stolen splendour on my throne?"

The goddess placed a soothing hand on his shoulder. "No, dear Odysseus. Your wife and son still loyally long for your return. But there are plenty of others who wish you dead and it is them you have to fear.

"Four years ago now the lords of Ithaca and nearby lands decided to give you up for dead. They agreed among themselves to compete for the hand of your wife, Penelope. You know well enough that she is held to be the loveliest woman, next to Helen herself, in the whole of Greece.

"Of course, few could hope to win the prize but many others have taken the opportunity to live in idle luxury at your expense. There are plenty of pretty serving maids to amuse them and they have eaten their way through your flocks and herds and drunk their way through your cellars without a thought to the future. For the suitors in your palace every day is a feast day. They are like a swarm of locusts. Unless Penelope chooses a new husband they have threatened to stay where they are until your cellars are empty and your fields are bare. Worse still, the suitors have already decided to kill your son, Telemachus, and share the kingdom out among themselves.

"With my help," Athene continued, "you will make sure that evil day never comes. Dearest of men, remember how I once stood by you on the dusty plains of Troy. In the thickest of the bloody battle I, Athene, protected you and gave you strength. For your wisdom and your cunning, for your courage and your beauty, you have long been my favourite among mortals. For almost ten years now I have been forced to stand by helplessly while my uncle, Poseidon, has pursued you across the seas. But I always knew you would survive and come home at last. Now you are here, I shall help you once again. But you must be patient and must be cunning.

"First I will disguise you as an old beggar. Then go to your swineherd, Eumaeus. He is as loyal as ever, but don't tell him who you are. It's safer that way. Meanwhile I will go to Sparta, where your son has gone to visit Menelaus, hoping to have news of you. He must return, now that you are here. The suitors plan to ambush him, but I will see to it that he is safe.

"Quickly now, let us hide your chest of treasures in the Naiads' cave before we go our separate ways."

When the chest was safely stowed away, the goddess touched Odysseus with her wand. At once his thick black hair turned thin and grey, his eyes dimmed. In exchange for Arete's fine purple tunic Athene gave him a cloak that was tattered and torn. Pleased with her work, she watched the stiff old beggar make his way inland. Then she set off for Sparta to find his son.

ODYSSEUS AND THE SWINEHERD

Odysseus climbed up from the beach and followed an old overgrown path through the woods. He had no need of directions. These were the woods and hills where he had played as a child and hunted wild boar as a young man. It was here, in early summer, that he used to gather wild strawberries with his mother's maids. But it was the late summer that he liked best, when, after weeks of suffocating heat, there were nights of rain. He would go out alone in the early morning mist, which hung, magically, waist-high above the ground, to meet the Dryads under the dripping branches. These woodland nymphs became his friends. They taught him the names of the flowers, trees and birds and showed him which of the myriad mushrooms that sprang up were poisonous and which were succulent and good to eat.

Odysseus knew these woods so well that he recognized each tree. The path was steep and uneven but he never faltered. It was only in appearance that Athene had changed him into an old beggar; underneath he was as strong as ever. Besides, each step he took gave him pleasure, for he was treading on his beloved Ithacan soil.

In the early afternoon he came out of the woods onto the open hills. Soon he could make out wisps of black smoke curling up over the swineherd's cottage. He hurried forward. It was just as he remembered twenty years before. Each stone, each fence-post was in its proper place and even the animals grazing in the paddock looked the same. But as he drew closer, four vicious-looking dogs rushed towards him, fangs bared. At once a familiar voice shouted above their bloodthirsty barking, commanding them to stop. The dogs slunk away from Odysseus, growling, disappointed. A man came running towards him. It was his swineherd, Eumaeus, and Odysseus was shocked to see the careworn face which made him look older than his years.

"Old man, forgive me," said Eumaeus. "I was busy cleaning out the sties with my men and didn't see you coming. I hate to keep these vicious hounds, but such are the times we live in. My master, Odysseus, has been gone these twenty years now and things are going from bad to worse. The palace is full of dissolute lords, and the young prince, Telemachus, can't control them. All sorts of unsavoury characters have come to Ithaca, and gangs roam the country-side to see what they can scrounge or steal. But enough of this. Come inside and let's see what I can offer you."

Eumaeus led Odysseus into his cottage and made him sit before the fire. Then he fetched a jug of rough red wine and a freshly slaugh-tered young hog which he spitted expertly and set to roast over the flames.

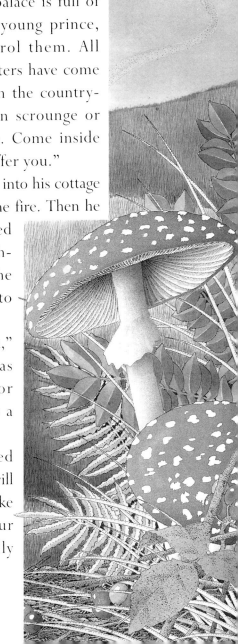

"May Zeus reward you," said Odysseus, as soon as Eumaeus sat down, "for your generous welcome to a wretched old beggar."

"Old friend," replied the swineherd, "it's the will of Zeus that we should take in whoever comes to our door in peace, especially those in need, and I can see that you've fallen on hard times. But instead of listening to my sorrows, which begin and end with the loss of dear Odysseus, my lord, tell me about yourself. Who are you? Where do you come from? And what brings you to this troubled land?"

Although it was only mid-afternoon it was dark as night in the windowless cottage. The two men sat close together in the flickering light of the fire. The wood smoke and the savour of the roasting pork made Odysseus' eyes and mouth water as he told Eumaeus his story.

Odysseus claimed to be a Cretan prince. As a young man he had won fame and fortune on the high seas. Then the call came to go to Troy. He joined the Achaean army with nine ships under his command and throughout those ten years of war he stood shoulder to shoulder with Odysseus and the rest. But on the voyage home everything had gone wrong. He lost his entire fleet and all the treasures he had won. He himself was captured and years of slavery followed, first in Egypt and then Phoenicia. Now, at long last, he had been set free, but he would not return to Crete in shame and had resolved to wander the world as a beggar until he died.

"If only I could reward your hospitality with

good news of your beloved master, my old friend Odysseus," he said as he ended his tale, "but I've heard nothing since we parted on the shores of Troy."

"It doesn't matter, old friend," replied Eumaeus, his eyes filling with tears. "I fear Odysseus died long ago, although I still pray for his return. But it does me good to talk of him and entertain his friend."

Dusk had fallen while the two men talked. Now they heard the squeals and grunts of the swine being herded into their pens for the night. Soon Eumaeus' four herdsmen came and joined them by the fire. While they devoured the remains of the roast pork, Eumaeus went to the sties and brought out the finest of all his hogs. He wanted to make a sacrifice to Zeus and to honour his guest. The herdsmen were weary from the day's work, but they sat up late that night, enjoying the delicious meat and the entrancing stories which Eumaeus and the stranger took turns to tell in the flickering shadows of the hearth.

When Eumaeus spoke of the suitors, bitter anger grew in Odysseus' heart. But he said nothing and it was easy to hide his feelings in the dimly-lit room. It was past midnight now and, in spite of the fire, a chill had penetrated the cottage.

Outside, the west wind whistled over the hills, driving before it an icy rain from off the sea. The feast was over and the men were ready to sleep. Wrapped only in threadbare rags, Odysseus began to shiver.

"Before we sleep," he said, as the men made to get up, "there's one more story I wish to tell. It concerns your noble king Odysseus and illustrates that quick-witted cunning which convinces me he's still alive. Unless the gods have destroyed him he will surely return, for no mortal could outwit him.

"We're all tired so I'll be brief. One night we crept across the dusty plains of Troy and hid in the reeds outside the city walls, ready to ambush the Trojan troops when they came out the following day. Odysseus, Menelaus and myself led a party of one hundred men. We made ourselves as comfortable as we could, in our heavy armour on the marshy ground, but the night was cold, the north wind blew and snow began to fall. I realized to my horror that I'd forgotten my cloak; dressed only in armour and my scanty tunic, I wouldn't survive the night. I turned to Odysseus, who lay beside me, to tell him of my plight. My lips were already blue with cold. Without a moment's hesitation he spoke to our men.

"Dear friends, we've managed to get here without being seen. Now someone must slip back to the camp to tell Agamemnon so that he's ready to draw the Trojans into our trap as soon as morning comes."

"Even before he'd finished speaking, Thoas, the best runner among us, leapt up and volunteered. He pulled off his purple cloak and let it fall to the ground as he ran off through the snow. Now I had a thick woollen cloak to keep me warm and so I survived the night."

Eumaeus chuckled softly. "Dear friend, your tale was well told and the point hasn't escaped me. Here, take my spare cloak. It'll keep you warm enough if you lie down on the goatskins by the fire. My men will stay here with you. I prefer to sleep outside in the old barn by the sties, in case there are any unwelcome visitors in the night."

Eumaeus wrapped himself up well and, as Odysseus watched him go, he felt a surge of warmth for this man who loved his lord so well.

FATHER AND SON

That same night, far away in Sparta, Telemachus lay awake while the rest of the household slept. The young prince tossed and turned uneasily in his bed. He had visited old King Nestor in Pylos, then travelled on to Sparta, where he was staying with Menelaus and Helen. Both great kings had welcomed him and treated him with honour for his father's sake, but neither knew what had happened to Odysseus since that fateful day when the Greek army sailed away from Troy. Telemachus was now convinced that his father must be dead and his troubled mind turned back to Ithaca. He would have to persuade his mother to marry one of the suitors before it was too late. Perhaps it was too late already.

Athene stood at his bedside watching, smiling to herself. He looked so like his father, her

favourite. Sensing her presence, the young prince sat up with a start.

"Don't be alarmed," she said, sitting down beside him. "I have come to tell you that you must return at once to Ithaca. The time is ripe. But you must be careful, for your mother's suitors have laid an ambush for you in the narrow straits between Ithaca and Samos. They intend to kill you and take all Ithaca for themselves. You must sail by night and slip ashore on the south coast, in the cove of Phorcys while your ship sails on to the city without you. Go straight to Eumaeus. You will be safe there, and you can send him to tell Penelope that you have returned. For the moment that is all you need to know." The goddess then wished Telemachus well and vanished into the night.

The young prince waited impatiently for dawn. At first light he hurried off along the dusty road to Pylos. Stopping only to change horses, he reached Pylos by nightfall and went straight to his ship where his crew was ready waiting. It was not long before the city lights had faded behind them. All that night the ship raced along the Peloponnesian coast, driven by a following wind. By dawn they were already passing Zacynthus and they reached the southern coast of Ithaca as darkness fell.

Meanwhile, Odysseus had passed two restful days, wandering the rugged hill tops, delighting in the land he knew and loved so well. In the evening he sat with Eumaeus by the fire and swapped more stories of the good old days. They talked of the present too and the more Odysseus learnt about the suitors, the more his heart hardened against them.

It was nearly midnight on the third evening and the other herdsmen were already fast asleep. Odysseus, in his beggar's disguise, sat before the blazing fire, still mulling over the past with Eumaeus. Outside the dogs only whined in greeting as the familiar young man made his way towards the cottage. Eumaeus and his guest jumped up in alarm when the door creaked open and a chilly draught swept across the room. The tall figure stepped in out of the moonlit night and closed the door safely behind him. Now Eumaeus leapt up and embraced him warmly. When they turned back towards him, Odysseus recognized his own features in the dimly-lit face of the new arrival.

"Dear Telemachus, thank the gods you're safe," said Eumaeus. "When I heard of your journey I was afraid that you'd never return, like your dear father. But what on earth brings you here? Is there any news?"

"No news, old friend, no news of the one thing that matters, although I've seen Menelaus and lovely Helen and I've talked with wise Nestor of my father's greatness and his glorious deeds. But only his bright memory remains; of the man himself I found no trace."

As Telemachus spoke, Odysseus got up to offer him his seat by the fire. The young prince took him gently by the arm and made him sit down again.

"No, no, old stranger, please. You're a guest in this house. For me it's a second home."

Telemachus squatted on his haunches in the hearth and warmed himself against the fire. Then he turned to Odysseus and examined him closely. Now tell me, old man, where are you from? What brings you here?"

Odysseus repeated the story he had told Eumaeus. When he had finished Telemachus looked downcast.

"It makes me so sad," he said quietly, staring at the fire, "to think that I can offer an old companion of my father's no better hospitality than this. You fought alongside my father on the dusty plains of Troy and no doubt he suffered as you did on the grim journey home. Perhaps he wandered the world like you and fell into captivity. Perhaps he still languishes in slavery in some distant land.

If that's the case I pray that death brings him an early release. As for myself, I've become a stranger in my father's palace. I'd like to invite you to enjoy its many comforts but I'm afraid you'd only suffer the derision of my mother's suitors."

"Noble prince," replied Odysseus, "your words are kind, but your concern is unnecessary. I'm so used to these rags which pass for clothes and the hard ground for my bed that the comforts of a palace would do little for me now. However, I'm sorry to hear of all your troubles. Have you no brothers or cousins who could help you drive these scroungers from your father's halls? I wish I were young enough for the fight or even that I were Odysseus himself. Then I'd destroy these evil men or die in the attempt. I'd sooner die, fighting for my rights, than suffer the daily humiliation which you endure."

"No, old man, I've no brothers; I come from a line of only sons. As for cousins, all the fine men who'd help me now went with my father to Troy. I hate the suitors and I'd love to see them get what they deserve, but it would be a foolish gesture to throw away my life in a hopeless cause. No, unless by some miracle Odysseus returns and together we can stand against these enemies, my mother will have to marry to rid our halls of them."

Odysseus was pleased with his son's wise answer, but he only stared into the fire and said not a word.

"And now, Eumaeus," said the young prince, "let me tell you why I'm here. The suitors hoped to kill me in an ambush before I got back to these shores, but, thanks to Athene, I was able to avoid them. I want you to go the palace and tell my mother I'm back, before I risk showing my face. If I'd disappeared without trace the suitors could have pretended they knew nothing about it, but I can't believe that even they'd dare kill me in broad daylight in front of my own people."

"Of course, dear Telemachus, I understand you perfectly. Should I pass by the farm on my way and tell old Laertes too? Since you left for Pylos his despair has doubled and he neither eats nor sleeps."

"No, go straight to the palace. I can't take any chances. Ask my mother to send her old house-keeper to my grandfather. Then come back here."

It was dawn. The stars had already faded in the early morning light and the sky was reddening in the east. Eumaeus threw another log on the fire and wrapped his thick cloak around him.

"I'll go at once," he said. "I'll be gone all day. Help yourselves to whatever you need."

Eumaeus slipped quietly out of the door and, in the same moment, the goddess Athene slipped in. She made herself visible to Odysseus alone and spoke in a voice that only he could hear.

"Odysseus, now is the time to reveal yourself. Tell your son everything. Tomorrow, go to the city and enter your palace. And remember, be as you always are, wise and bold. I will be close by."

Before she left, the goddess touched the old beggar with her wand. At once his back straightened and his skin was made taut and smooth. His dim eyes brightened and his thin grey hair turned thick and black. In place of his rags he wore Arete's purple tunic once again.

Telemachus looked up and paled. "Stranger, you must be a god. I pray that you've come in a friendly spirit."

"Telemachus, don't be afraid of me for I'm no god. Come closer and see how alike we are. And so we should be, for my name is Odysseus and you're my dear son."

And with those words he threw his arms around Telemachus and held him close. Great sobs welled up from both men and the father's

tears mingled with the son's as they ran freely down their faces. Then, they stood back and examined each other. They laughed with joy to see how alike they were.

They sat down before the fire, all thought of sleep forgotten, and started to tell each other of their lives. Odysseus told his son about the years in Troy and the story of his unlucky journey home. When at last he finished, the young prince had laughed and cried a hundred times.

In the early afternoon they took a skin of wine and a basket of food and walked to a spot they both knew, high on the hillside above the swineherd's cottage. Sheltered among large rocks, they could look out across the island to the city, while Telemachus told his father of his childhood and his early youth and what had happened since the suitors came. Later, as the sun was going down behind the hills, they turned their minds to the present.

"Dear son," said Odysseus, "listen well to what I have to say. The suitors are many and we are just two. But I promise you this: with our strength and guile and the help of Athene, we'll destroy them all. Tomorrow go back to the palace. Say nothing about me, not even to your mother. I'll follow in my beggar's disguise. The suitors will abuse me. Say nothing. When it's time to strike I'll tell you. Now we must return to the cottage for Eumaeus will be back soon. And one last thing, whenever you're afraid, remember to trust in me."

"Dear Father, alone I was afraid, but now that you're here I've the courage of a hundred men. If Zeus and Athene are with us then the suitors are surely doomed."

THE BEGGAR COMES TO TOWN

The suitors were worried. The young prince had outwitted them and the queen had accused them of his attempted murder. They laughed off her accusation as the ravings of a troubled mind, but they were alarmed by the turn events had taken. Now they sat uneasily in the great hall of the palace, pondering their next move.

"I'm all for finding the boy and finishing the job off properly," said Antinous. "As long as he's alive we'll never get our way."

"But we should choose our time carefully," said Eurymachus. "We must make it look like an accident. There's no need to kill him in broad daylight. For the moment let's just watch and wait."

The other suitors murmured their assent. There were a few, like Amphinomus, who felt that what they were doing was wrong, but they were powerless to oppose Antinous and Eurymachus. These two ruthless men had become the suitors' spokesmen and leaders. They effectively ran the palace. After three years in Ithaca, most of the suitors had abandoned any ambitions to marry

Penelope themselves and were content to enjoy themselves as privileged followers and hangers-on.

Hardly had they agreed to postpone his murder when Telemachus himself entered the hall. A hush fell over the suitors as they watched the young prince approach. His face was pale as death and his voice trembled with anger and contempt. "Is it such a shock, then, to see me back in my own house? Or were you expecting to see my ghost?"

"My dear Telemachus," replied Eurymachus in honeyed tones, "I can't tell you what a relief it is to see you again. We were afraid that you were lost on the high seas like your father."

"Telemachus, welcome home," said Antinous, stepping forward to place a hand on the young prince's shoulder. "And now that you're back let me offer you some fatherly advice – after all, I hope to be your father soon. Your lovely mother's been ill with worry since you went away. We've done everything in our power to comfort her but she still fears the worst. Go to her. Ask her to forgive you for all the trouble you've caused."

Telemachus angrily shook off the treacherous suitor's hand. He walked out of the hall without a word and climbed the stairs to Penelope's lonely room. He found his mother lying on her bed,

weeping for her long-lost husband and the bleak future which stared her in the face. When she saw her son she leapt up and embraced him. It was a long time before either of them spoke. Then, when Penelope grew calm, they sat on the edge of her bed and Telemachus told her about his journey. She questioned him closely and he kept nothing back, except the most important news of all. He longed to tell her that Odysseus was already in Ithaca, less than a day's walk from the palace, but he had sworn silence. She would know soon enough.

In fact even now, as mother and son were talking, Odysseus stood before the palace gates, He and Eumaeus had set out from the swineherd's cottage that same morning and he had already had a taste of what lay in store for him. Not far from the city they had encountered Melanthius, the royal goatherd, driving a dozen of his best goats to the palace to please the greedy suitors. Melanthius considered the swineherd his rival and resented his loyalty to Odysseus. He himself had sided with the suitors from the start. Seeing Eumaeus in the company of a miserable beggar, the goatherd laughed out loud.

"Well, you two are well-matched, I must say. I hope you're not taking your new friend to the palace, Eumaeus. The suitors don't care for mangy dogs. They treat them like this."

And Melanthius kicked Odysseus hard in the side as he passed him. Odysseus winced and stumbled. His first impulse was to punish the arrogant goatherd there and then. Instead, like a real old beggar, he shrunk away from his attacker and stared at the ground.

Eumaeus was white with fury. "You might laugh now, Melanthius, and strut about like a suitor while your herds are steadily eaten away. But I promise you this, you'll dance to different tune when Odysseus returns."

Melanthius laughed even louder. "You too Eumaeus, you're like an old dog that's lost its master. Don't you understand, Odysseus will never come back now. Either he's six feet under in some unknown land or keeping company with the flat fish at the bottom of the sea. And a good thing too if you ask me. I like the suitors and they like me. The trouble with you is that you're stuck in your ways and too proud to make yourself useful. So, while I sit among the lords and princes, you go around with a flea-ridden old beggar."

Melanthius swaggered on ahead while Odysseus bit his lip and watched him go. Eumaeus sighed and shook his head. The two men walked on in silence, each of them deep in thought. Before long they entered the city and soon the palace itself came into view.

Odysseus stood before the palace gates and gazed in wonder at his home. On the outside at least, nothing had changed. A soft whine caught his attention and he looked down to see an ancient hunting dog which lay wheez-ing in the shade of a steaming dunghill beside the gates. The dog was half-starved and cov-ered in sores, but Odysseus could tell that it had once been a fine animal. It stared up at him, twitching its ears

and feebly wagging its tail. Suddenly, in its ruined features he recognized Argos, his favourite dog which he had reared himself, from a tiny puppy, all those years before. He knelt down and gently patted its head, forcing back the tears so that Eumaeus would not see.

"Come, old friend," said Eumaeus. "The young prince has asked me to bring you to the palace and here we are. Leave that poor creature and follow me. And I warn you, be prepared for some rough treatment. Like most cowards who hunt in packs, these precious suitors are cruel men."

The swineherd led the way through the gates towards the great hall and the old beggar hobbled close behind him. Neither of them looked back to see the old dog breathe its last, happy to die now that it had seen Odysseus again.

Inside the great hall Odysseus was shocked by the scene that met his eyes. Men lay about everywhere, gorging themselves on roast meat and swilling back strong red wine. The air was full of raucous shouts and drunken laughter. Some of

Penelope's maids sat with the men, giggling at the crude jokes and flirting openly. At the far end of the hall, a little apart from the rest, Telemachus shared a table with a few trusted friends: ancient Halitherses, Peiraeus, Medon the page and Phemius the bard. The young prince called Eumaeus over while Odysseus, in his beggar's disguise, sat just inside the threshold and waited.

Soon Eumaeus returned with bread and meat from the young prince's table. Odysseus chewed his food slowly, considering his next move. Setting his meal aside, he stepped out of the shadows and moved among the suitors with an outstretched hand. Most of them ignored him, but Antinous jumped up angrily at his approach.

"Insolent swineherd," he hissed, turning to Eumaeus, "how dare you bring a vermin-infested creature like this into our midst? You complain often enough that we devour your young master's inheritance. Do you expect us to share it with this dirty old beggar? Get the wretch out of here before I drag him out and throw him to the dogs."

The other suitors roared their approval. It would be good sport to set the dogs on this old beggar even though he wouldn't last long. But when Telemachus stood up to face Antinous they fell silent. The young prince's face was grim and his voice was cold with anger. "Antinous, aren't you satisfied to live at my expense? Would you instruct me how to live as well? Leave the old man alone or you'll pay for your cruelty."

Antinous was too astonished to reply. Telemachus had never dared speak out like this. Odysseus seized the chance to provoke him further.

"Come then, noble lord," he said, stretching out his hand again, "will you not give me something now? Or are you too mean to spare the crumbs from another man's table?"

"Old fool," answered Antinous, "I'll give you something all right, to repay your insults as they deserve."

And he grabbed a footstool and hurled it at Odysseus, hitting him full in the chest with a sickening thud. The old beggar staggered back and almost fell. Without another glance at Antinous he shook his head sadly and walked back to his place by the main doors. Fierce anger surged up in his son's heart but, wisely, he bit his lip and held back his hand. It was not yet time.

The hall fell strangely quiet. The old beggar had upset the party and no one knew quite what to make of it.

However, it was not long before something happened which made every one forget the incident. A well-known Ithacan beggar, called Irus, who regarded the palace as his own territory, had just got wind of his rival's presence. Now he appeared in the doorway, determined to drive the trespasser away. He gave Odysseus a sharp kick in the ribs and shouted at him so that the whole hall could hear.

"Clear out of here, old man, or I'll kick you out. This is my patch. I've been begging here for years and I'm treated like one of the family."

"I've got just as much right to be here as you," replied Odysseus. "Besides, there's plenty to go round. But I warn you, don't be deceived by my appearance. I've fought and beaten many better men than you in my long life."

The suitors laughed gleefully at the sight of the two beggars challenging each other to a fight. Now they would have some fun. They led them out to the courtyard and formed a large circle round them. Then they stripped off their rags. When Irus saw his opponent's muscular body he stepped back trembling, but it was too late to back down. The fight didn't last long. Within seconds Irus lay in the dust with blood streaming from his nose. The suitors left him propped up, semi-conscious, against the courtyard wall and carried Odysseus back into the hall on their shoulders, in mock triumph. Then they drank to him as a champion.

"This must be a god among beggars," sneered Eurymachus, "See how the light shines on his bald head. What a pity he's allowed himself to degenerate into a cringing parasite. If he was willing to use those strong limbs to work instead of beg, I'd pay him well. As it is, the only thing about him that really works is his fat belly."

"Eurymachus," replied the beggar king, "you're the parasite, so bloated with conceit that you find it easier to insult others than exert yourself. I beg because I have to, and if I had the chance to swing a scythe or guide a plough then you'd see what I could do. But it's clear that your brain, like your smooth white hands, has never been properly used. You and Antinous think you're great lords because all these other dogs fawn at your heels. But I warn you, Eurymachus, when the lion returns to his lair you'll die like a dog with the rest of them. You'll run yelping from Odysseus' vengeance, and there'll be nowhere to hide."

"Insolent old fool!" snarled Eurymachus. "You

must be drunk or crazy to speak to me like that. Antinous clearly had the right idea. Here's some more of his medicine."

The stool was aimed straight at Odysseus's head, but he ducked beneath it and it crashed into the wine-bearer standing behind him. The wine-bearer buckled at the knees, dropping his jar. The blood-red wine splashed across the marble floor. There was uproar in the hall.

"This wretched old beggar has brought nothing but trouble," said a suitor, raising his voice above the general commotion.

"If he stays here any longer we'll be at each other's throats," said another. "Let's throw him out before it's too late."

"Then you'll have to throw me out too," said Telemachus, placing himself in front of his disguised father. "It seems to me that it's all of you who have had too much to drink, not this poor old man. I suggest you go and sleep it off. After all, tomorrow is Apollo's feast day and I'm sure you all need a good rest to get back your appetites."

The suitors were astonished to hear the young prince speak to them so sternly. But they were not inclined to argue. For the first time in over three years they felt unsure of their ground.

It had been a very disturbing day.

THE BEGGAR AND
THE QUEEN

The suitors had departed, some to their homes in the city and others to their beds in the palace. Odysseus and his son were at last alone in the great hall.

"We must move quickly now," said Odysseus. "Athene has warned me that tomorrow's the day of reckoning. The suitors will be married at last and their bride will be grim death."

He waved an arm around the walls. Everywhere hung swords and spears, helmets and armour. "Clear all these away and hide them in one of the store-rooms. If anyone asks what's happened to them, say that they were tarnished and you sent them to be cleaned. And hide enough weapons for ourselves in the corner by the door. When you've finished go straight to bed and try to get some sleep. I'll spend the night here in front of the fire."

The walls were quickly cleared and soon Odysseus was left alone. Meanwhile, Penelope had heard about the stranger and she longed to talk with him. Perhaps, by some miracle, he brought news of her husband. When she was sure that the loathsome suitors had gone, she went down to the hall where her maids, as they did every night, were clearing up after her would-be husbands. The stranger, a curiously familiar-looking, sad-faced old beggar, was sitting in the glow of the fire. Little suspecting that this old man in rags was her long-lost husband, Penelope drew up a chair beside him.

"Old stranger, you are welcome to my hearth. Please tell me who you are. Eumaeus has told me something of you. And I now long to hear your story from your own lips."

Odysseus stared into the fire. His wife's voice made his flesh melt. When, at last, he turned his face towards her, a single tear rolled down his old man's cheek. "Noble queen, forgive me. I'm afraid you must think me a pathetic old man, but when I remember all that I've lost I can't hold back my tears."

"Old friend," answered Penelope, with a sad smile, "I'm no stranger to sorrow myself. For twenty years now

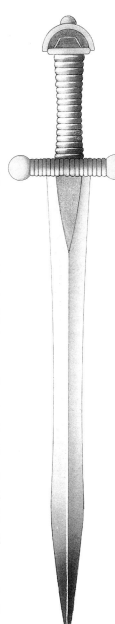

I've waited for the man I love. Every night I've soaked my pillow with fresh tears. For more than three years I've been besieged by suitors who ruin this house and eat away my heart. Not one of them is fit to wash my husband's feet. When they first came I asked them to wait until I'd finished weaving a shroud for Laertes, my husband's dear father. It was a duty to which they could hardly object. Each day I'd weave and each night I'd secretly unravel all my work. I spun this out for more than three years until one of my maids betrayed me. The suitors were understandably furious, and now I can put them off no longer.

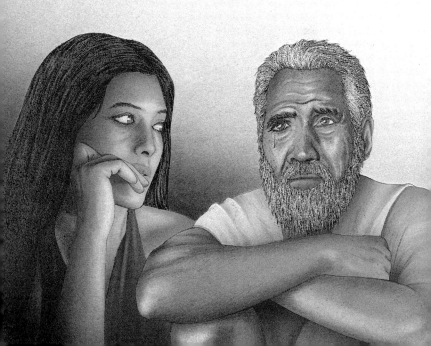

"Oh, how I curse the name of Ilium! Odysseus never wanted to go to Troy. We were deeply in love and our son was only days old when the call came. Odysseus knew it would be a long war, a pointless war for petty pride, and he knew he might never return. He told me to look after his kingdom and to care for his father and mother. And if he'd not returned when Telemachus came of age, then I should marry again. Old friend, tomorrow I shall make my choice, though it will break my heart."

Odysseus wanted to reach out to Penelope and tell her he was home, but he knew he must not weaken now. He could not expect her to hide her feelings after so long. After twenty years, they could surely wait one more day.

"Noble queen," he said, "your deep sorrow matches my own. If only I brought good news, if only I could say that any day now your husband will return in glory to his home. I can't. I know too well what it's like to have hopes raised then cruelly dashed away. But tell me, if you can bear to speak of it, how you're going to make your choice, for I'm curious to know your plans."

"Gladly, old friend, and since you've the air of a wise counsellor you can tell me whether you approve. My husband had a favourite bow which he left behind when he went to Troy. He was a great archer, and I still remember how his face lit up each time he took this bow in his hands. He loved to use it and show off his skill. You know the tiny brass rings that are used to hang ceremonial axes on the wall? Well, Odysseus would line up twelve axes with their handles in the air and fire his arrows through the rings. It was a remarkable feat. Others who tried couldn't even string the bow. Tomorrow I'll bring this bow and line up twelve axes in the hall. Whoever strings the bow and shoots an arrow through the rings will win my hand. If none succeeds then I'll marry the first man to string the bow."

"Noble Queen, your plan's a good one. If I were younger, I'd ask to try your husband's bow myself. Not, I need hardly add, as a suitor for your hand. I'm not yet such an old fool as that. But I love archery and, I have to admit, I'd love to see the suitors' faces if a miserable old beggar were to show them up."

Penelope laughed. "That would be a sight worth seeing. And if you want to I'll make sure you get the chance. But now, old friend, you've listened to my tale of sorrow long enough. My women will bathe you and bring you fresh clothes and bedding and then I'll leave you to sleep."

"Dear queen, for many years I've dressed in

rags and made my bed on the hard ground. I'm an old man and it's too late to change my habits now. Clean linen and a soft bed would be wasted on me. Besides, I wouldn't like these young women to touch my wrinkled skin. But perhaps that old woman who stands beside you might wash my aching feet; from the sadness in her eyes I can see that she too has known great sorrow in her life."

Odysseus was looking at Eurycleia, his old nurse who was now the closest companion of Penelope's sorrow.

"I'll do it gladly," said Eurycleia, "for dear Penelope's sake and for your own. And for the sake of my dear Odysseus too. For although you're worn and bowed down by age and sorrow, you look just as he'd have looked had he lived to be as old as you."

The old nurse warmed a basin of water on the blazing fire and set it down at the beggar's feet. As she washed him her fingers touched an old scar running up his right thigh from above the knee. She peered at it closely with her dim old eyes, then let go of his leg so suddenly that his foot dropped into the basin with a splash. Odysseus looked round in alarm, but no one was watching.

"Odysseus, my darling child," exclaimed Eurycleia, "You've come home to us at last! That scar's an old friend of mine. Remember how many times I changed the dressing on that dreadful wound?"

When he was still a boy, Odysseus had been wounded by a boar in the woods of Parnassus. It was a deep gash and he had been carried back to the palace where Eurycleia had nursed the wound until it healed. Now, in the joy of recognition, the old nurse turned to Penelope to share the good news. Before she could utter a sound Odysseus had gripped her sharply by the wrist and pulled her towards him.

"Dear nurse, this is indeed Odysseus who sits before you. But don't think I come disguised for amusement's sake. This is no time for games. If the suitors discover that I'm here, they'll kill me like a dog. They've already agreed to carve up my kingdom between them and they've spent too long here to give up now."

"My child," replied Eurycleia, "your secret's safe with me. Remember I once nursed you at my breast. And, if there's any justice in this world, then I'll live to see you drive the cruel suitors from your land and set our people free."

"That, old nurse, is in the hands of the gods. Let's pray that they're on my side."

Eurycleia continued to bathe the old beggar's feet and legs in silence. When she had finished,

Penelope wished her guest goodnight and climbed the stairs to her lonely room in the company of her maids. Now Odysseus sat alone in the great hall, staring into the glowing heart of the fire. After all that he had been through his greatest test was still to come. And it would come tomorrow.

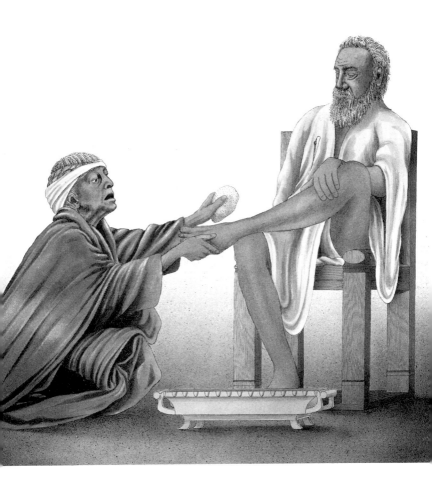

THE CONTEST OF THE BOW

It was Apollo's feast day and in the royal palace preparations began at dawn. The old beggar sat unnoticed in a quiet corner of the courtyard and watched the procession of animals and wagons laden with olives and corn file through the city streets. Most of these were taken to the temple to be offered to Apollo in public sacrifice, but many of the choicest cattle, sheep and swine were drawn aside and brought to the palace for the enjoyment of the greedy suitors. A grim smile played across the old beggar's lips. If Athene stood by him their enjoyment would indeed be short-lived.

At midday the suitors began to drift away from the public ceremony back to the palace. They gathered in the courtyard, just outside the great hall, and soon their laughter filled the air. They were looking forward to the feast and nobody mentioned the disturbing scenes of the day before. They had been forgotten, like a bad dream.

As Odysseus watched them from his corner in the shadows a small group drew aside from the rest and walked in his direction. It was the inner circle of suitors led by Antinous and Eurymachus. They stopped, only a few metres from him, and huddled together, conferring in low voices. None of them noticed the old beggar, who sat still as a stone and heard every

word of their plan to murder Telemachus that very night when the whole city would be caught up in festive celebrations.

They quickly agreed on the details; Antinous told them what needed to be done. Then they rejoined the main group of suitors and entered the great hall. Odysseus waited long enough for the feast to get under way before he followed them in. Strong wine was already flowing freely and he was greeted by a chorus of groans and jeers.

"Why, if it isn't our mysterious old friend," said Ctesippus, one of Antinous' cronies. "Here, have a drink, old man."

Ctesippus offered Odysseus a bowl of wine. As he stretched out a hand to take it, Ctesippus pulled the bowl aside and poured the contents over his head. Red wine ran down his face and neck, soaking his tattered rags. The hall echoed to the suitors' cheers and laughter.

"Here's some food to go with your wine," a voice shouted and a half-chewed bone hit Odysseus on the shoulder. Soon a volley of missiles came at him from all directions and pieces of bread, meat, tomato and olive clung to his skin and clothes. Ctesippus staggered back to his place, doubled up with laughter.

Now it was the turn of Leocritus, another of

the inner circle, to lead the fun. "Old man, this is the second day that you've enjoyed our charity in this hall. It's time you showed us a little gratitude by entertaining us. Come on, old beggar, we know you can eat and drink all right. Now let's see you dance and sing."

The suitors bayed and whooped in mock encouragement. Odysseus gazed slowly round the hall, taking in each of their flushed, fleshy faces. He did not bother to conceal his contempt.

"Hurry up, old man," said Leocritus, "there's no need to be coy. If you're suffering from stage fright perhaps you'd better have another drink."

He picked up a bowl of wine from the table and swaggered towards Odysseus. The other suitors roared him on, pounding on the tables with their fists.

"Enough," cried Telemachus fiercely. He leapt between Leocritus and his father, grabbed the suitor's wrist and dashed the bowl to the ground.

"Aren't you ashamed of yourselves," he demanded, looking round the hall, "abusing this poor old beggar so cruelly? Leave him alone and get on with your feast. The next man to disgrace this hall will answer to my sword."

The young prince led his father to his own table and set food and wine before him. Now

Antinous got to his feet. His face was pale and he shook with rage.

"No, Telemachus, it is we who've had enough – of this wretched beggar's impudence and your ill-chosen words. This may be your father's palace but we're your elders and betters and you should treat us with respect. I'm warning you, young man, if you get in our way it'll be the worse for you. We'll do as we like and there's nothing that you or your dear mother can do to stop us."

An uneasy silence fell over the hall as Antinous and the young prince stood facing each other. Then Athene, who sat invisible at the far end of the hall, decided to intervene. She mesmerized the suitors, who began to laugh and cry uncontrollably. Their faces were twisted and paralysed and the roast meat on their plates turned raw and began to bleed. Odysseus and his son gazed at the scene in amazement. Outside, the afternoon turned black as night and, while tears streamed down the suitors' frozen faces and strangled laughter came gurgling from their throats, small streams of blood oozed from the corners of their mouths and trickled slowly down their chins.

Odysseus spoke and broke the spell. "Godless men, can't you see the signs? Your day's turned into night and your blood's begun to flow."

The suitors had returned to their senses but remembered nothing of their trance. Eurymachus laughed contemptuously at Odysseus. "Oh, you men of Greece, listen to the prophet speak. Is this the thanks we are to get for our charity? An old fool foretelling our doom. Since he thinks it's so dark in here let's kick him out into the blazing sun!"

But before his words had died away Penelope entered the hall and the old beggar was forgotten. The queen was dressed in a dazzling robe and flanked by six maids carrying twelve axes and blocks. Penelope herself carried a quiverful of arrows and a magnificent bow.

"Arrogant suitors," she began in a trembling voice, "your day has come at last. You've wallowed in this house for four years now, growing fat on our food and loud and stupid on our wine and you've given nothing in return. Your excuse has been that you wish to marry me, in spite of the fact that my husband might still be alive. Well, here's your chance to win the prize. Whoever can string Odysseus' bow and shoot an arrow through a line of twelve axe-heads will take me from this palace as his wife. Good Eumaeus, set the bow down before the suitors and you, my dear Telemachus, help me arrange these axes as your dear father used to all those years ago."

They lined up the blocks and stood the axes in them. The brass rings on the handle tips glistened in the dim light of the hall. The young prince was fired by the sight of his father's famous bow and the desire to prove himself a worthy son. He flung off his purple cloak, took the bow from his mother and carried it over to the steps in front of the threshold where he made a mark for the contestants to stand behind. Then he knelt down and examined the target carefully. The line of axes was straight and true. Telemachus fitted the string into the notch at one end of the bow and began to bend it with his knees. It was hard work but he sensed at once that he would master it. He was interrupted by a dry cough from the shadows beside him and, looking round, he caught his father's warning eye. Telemachus laid down the bow.

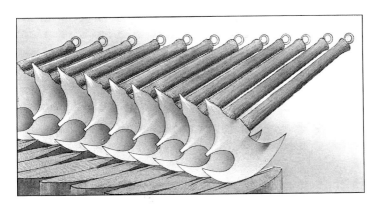

"It seems that I'm still too young and weak to string my father's bow," he said, walking back to his seat. "In any case this contest's not for me. Come now, you mighty suitors, let's see who's man enough to win my mother's hand."

A heated argument immediately broke out. To most of the suitors it seemed a simple enough thing to string a bow and shoot straight. They had whiled away many hours of their four idle years in Ithaca with archery competitions and could handle a bow and arrow with considerable skill. The difficulty of the present contest, so they thought, lay in getting their hands on the bow in the first place. There were more than a hundred suitors in all. Since the first to succeed would win the prize, then the first to go had the best chance of winning. Surely this made the contest no better than a lottery?

It was Antinous who solved the problem. He suggested that they follow the order in which the wine was ceremonially poured. Since Antinous would be last, according to this system, no one could reasonably object. The other suitors applauded him and praised his generosity. They little realized that he thought going last gave him the best chance of success. He had seen at once that this was no ordinary bow and that few of them had a hope of even stringing it, especially as it had lain unused for twenty years. The more it was tried, the more supple it should become.

One by one the suitors stepped up to the mark and one by one they returned to their places defeated. Finally only Eurymachus and Antinous were left. Eurymachus stepped forward first.

He attached the string to the bottom notch and used all his weight to bend the bow down. For a moment it looked as if he might succeed but when he got half-way the bow would give no further. He struggled until he was red in the face and the sweat poured off his brow, all to no avail. Cursing under his breath he flung the bow to the ground.

Now Antinous stepped forward eagerly, sure of success. The bow he could not bend had yet to be made. But the smile soon faded from his lips. He could do no better than the others. Unwilling to accept defeat he called for grease, which he then worked into the wood to make the bow more supple. When he had warmed it in front of the fire, he tried again; it still would not bend. Eurymachus too tried the bow again, without success. The suitors hung their heads and a sense of despair descended on them all.

"We mustn't be dismayed," said Antinous,

anxious to lift the gloom. "Today's the feast day of Apollo, god of archery. No doubt it was foolish of us to think we could bend this bow on such a day. Let's put it aside and try again tomorrow. And let's drink to Apollo to win the god's approval."

The wine flowed and within minutes their failure was forgotten. Antinous was surely right. It was not the day for archery.

All the while Odysseus sat in the shadows, biding his time. He had seen his bow defeat the suitors and now he was ready to turn it against them. If Athene was with him they would never see another day.

"Noble lords," he said, stepping out into the centre of the hall, "Antinous is right. Apollo's feast day is the wrong day for such a contest. If he's willing, tomorrow will bring a different result. But I hope no one will object if I try the bow myself. Many years ago I owned a bow just like this one. It was my pride and joy and it would give a poor old man harmless pleasure to handle such a bow again."

"Insolent old fool," replied Eurymachus angrily, "we should have thrown your rotting carcass to the dogs yesterday when you first opened your mouth. How can you presume to do what so many strong young men could not? And, if by some miracle or freak of nature you were to succeed, do you think the rest of us would suffer the humiliation in silence? You'd be torn apart before you could reach the door. And do you think Penelope would marry a vermin-infested old man like you?"

At these harsh words Penelope rose from her seat and stood at the old man's side. "It makes me laugh, Eurymachus, to hear you speak of humiliation. Where does this sense of honour suddenly spring from? You've managed to hide it well enough for the past four years. What makes you want to introduce it now? In any case, this poor old man isn't like you. He doesn't ask to marry me. He merely wants to try my husband's bow. Let him do as he likes with it. If he succeeds where all you brave young men have failed, then I shall give him rich gifts and fine clothes so that he can return to his native land with honour instead of wandering the earth in shame and sorrow until he dies."

"My mother's right," agreed Telemachus. "Let the old man have his way. It can do no harm. And now, dear mother, why don't you go to your room and rest? The contest is over for today and you look suddenly tired and drawn."

Penelope was grateful. She had been under

such strain that she was in danger of falling ill. She left the hall with her maids at her side, glad to have won another day's reprieve. As she made her way upstairs the old nurse, Eurycleia, silently dropped behind and bolted the inner doors of the great hall from the outside. Now there was only one way out, across the main threshold.

Odysseus walked up to the mark and picked up the great bow. He weighed it lovingly, running his hands gently over the seasoned willow. It may have hung unused for twenty years but he could tell at once that its condition was perfect. The suitors watched him and laughed.

"Well, well," sneered Antinous, "I see our old beggar's something of a connoisseur of bows. Perhaps he's memorizing the design so that he can go away and make one for himself."

"He's certainly got more chance of making one than stringing one," said Leocritus.

"Oh come, come," said Eurymachus, "can't you see he's a veritable Apollo among beggars."

Odysseus ignored the mockery. He tested the bow in his hands, taking his time, until it began to feel once more, as it had done all those years ago, like an extension of his own arms and hands. At last he was satisfied and, in a single flowing movement, he bent it back and strung it and then plucked it like a lyre so that it sang out pure and clear as a swallow's song. Before the solitary note had faded in the air a single peal of thunder came from the heavens in reply. The suitors stared at the beggar open-mouthed as he pulled a long slender arrow from the quiver at his feet, turned to the line of axes and took aim. The arrow sped clean through the rings and buried itself, quivering, in the wall beyond.

THE DEATH OF THE SUITORS

There was a stunned silence in the hall. All eyes were on Odysseus. He seized the quiverful of arrows, leapt up the steps onto the threshold and turned to face the suitors with Telemachus at his side. Behind them the great doors were already barred. Then, with the suitors still frozen in their seats, Odysseus took aim again and sent a second arrow flying across the hall. It sank deep into Antinous' throat. The cruel suitor fell dying to the floor, blood spurting from the wound.

Immediately the hall was in an uproar. The suitors shouted angrily at the beggar. He had killed the noblest lord in Ithaca and he would pay for it with his life. But when they turned to the walls for weapons they saw to their dismay that they had all been removed. They looked back at the beggar with the bow and their hearts began to tremble.

It seemed to them that the old man in rags had turned into a god. Perhaps it was Apollo himself.

"You slavering dogs," said Odysseus, "well might you cower and cringe with fear, for the lion has returned. You thought I was gone forever and that you could do as you pleased in my house. If you'd come here with dignity and honour I'd gladly have forgiven you and you'd have welcomed my return. But you've lived a life of idle luxury and shame at my expense. You've terrorized my family and my servants and mocked at their suffering. You've lived as cruel cowards and you'll die like dogs."

"Noble Odysseus, listen to me please," broke in Eurymachus, in a smooth, pleading voice. "Listen before you start a bloodbath in your hall. It's true that we've behaved badly here and done things we all regret. But what can you expect from high-spirited young men? Remember you were once young yourself. Besides, the worst culprit is already dead, lying in his own blood at our feet. It was Antinous who wanted to kill your son and take over your kingdom for himself. He was an evil man and we were afraid of him. He deserved to die; let the rest of us make amends. We'll repay twice over all that we've taken here."

Odysseus gave a bitter laugh. "Eurymachus, even if you gave me everything you have, that wouldn't be enough. You're a liar and a thief like the dead dog at your feet and neither you nor any of the rest will leave this hall alive."

When he heard these words Eurymachus realized that they would have to fight their way out. Now, instead of pleading, he snarled back at Odysseus. "Arrogant fool, you don't stand a chance. There are more than a hundred of us here and we have followers all over the city. You've only your puny son and that obstinate old swineherd. What a pity that you should have come home at last only to die in your own hall."

Eurymachus ran straight at Odysseus with his sword raised above his head. The arrow passed clean through his heart and stopped him dead. He collapsed sideways across a table and his dark blood mingled with spilt red wine as it dripped onto the floor.

The suitors rushed towards the threshold, swords drawn, with tables held in front of them to shield them against the rain of deadly arrows. They shouted and cursed to give themselves courage. But Odysseus and his son stood firm with Athene watching over them. The goddess make sure that each arrow found its mark and gave Telemachus extra strength as he held the suitors off with spear and sword. When the arrows had run out, father and son stood side-by-side and cut a swathe through the suitors whose corpses piled up on the marble floor.

Meanwhile Eumaeus, who had been hurling javelins past Odysseus and his son into the advancing mass, caught sight of his old enemy Melanthius, struggling to open one of the inner doors at

the far end of the hall. With a fierce cry he dashed towards him and drove a spear through his body deep into the door beyond. The goatherd writhed like a harpooned fish and Eumaeus left him there to die slowly, while the suitors, who could not save him now, were slaughtered before his eyes.

It did not last long. Athene was with them and no one could resist. Father and son rested on their swords and paused for breath. More than a hundred corpses lay around them. Odysseus was covered from head to foot in blood and gore. He looked about him and caught sight of two figures crouched beneath one of the tables, partly concealed by the pile of bodies. So two of the cowardly suitors thought they could escape his vengeance. He went towards them, sword raised, ready to finish his bloody task.

A slight figure crawled out from under the table and clasped him by the knees. It was Phemius the bard. Once Odysseus had loved this man for his music and song, but now he was ready to kill him for he had found him with the suitors. As he raised the blood-stained sword above his head, Telemachus grasped him by the arm.

"No, father, spare him; I'd sooner you killed me first. He's as innocent as the very hills and trees. When the suitors came he wanted to leave rather than sing for them. It was I who persuaded him to stay. I told him that one day you'd surely return and that he should be here to welcome you with his song."

While Telemachus spoke the other figure emerged and knelt before them. It was Medon the page.

"Get up, Medon, you've nothing to fear. My father is vengeful but he's also just. When I tell him how you looked after me in my childhood and protected me from the scheming suitors for so long, I'm sure that he'll reward you with his love and not his sword."

"My son is right," agreed Odysseus, smiling now. "Medon and Phemius, I see that you have been dear friends to him as you always were to me. Later we'll sit together and talk about old times. But now let's clear these bodies from the hall and wash this blood away."

They called for Eurycleia and the maids, who unbolted the inner doors and entered the hall. The old nurse rejoiced when she saw what had happened but Odysseus restrained her. Bloodshed and death were no cause for celebration. The maids were sickened by the carnage that met their eyes. Some wept bitter tears, for the men who had become their lovers lay among the dead.

It took them a long time to empty the hall. Odysseus was anxious to conceal what had happened until he had time to prepare, for many of the suitors had family and friends in the city. So they carried the bodies through a side door into the rear courtyard, where Medon and Eumaeus burned them on a fire. The smell of burning flesh would cause no comment on a great feast day when the city air was heavy with the smell of sacrificial fires.

When, at long last, they had cleared the hall and scraped and scrubbed it clean, Odysseus sent the old nurse to fetch his wife. She found her in a deep and dreamless sleep and shook her hard to wake her. Penelope thought that the old nurse must have gone mad.

"Old Eurycleia, how can what you say be true? My husband was a great man but even he could not have stood alone against so many."

However, to humour her, Penelope went down with her to the hall. When she saw Odysseus she stepped back in amazement, trembling and pale. Her husband stood before her exactly as she remembered him. It was as though his twenty years' absence had been nothing but a dream.

"Dear mother," said Telemachus, "are you so heartless that you have nothing to say to my father, who has come home after so long and so much suffering?"

"Dear son, I can't believe my eyes. This must be some god who wears my husband's shape and form. I dare not believe, after so long, that it's really him. My heart aches and my mind is numbed at the sight of him. Go, Telemachus, and all the rest of you. Leave us here alone. If this is indeed Odysseus, then I shall soon know him for myself."

Now husband and wife were alone. Still trembling, Penelope approached Odysseus. She ran a hand down his leg and found the scar she knew so well. Then she looked up at him and spoke.

"Odysseus, unlucky wanderer, can it really be you? Should I tell the maids to bring out our bed and make it up once more? When you left me twenty years ago I had it put away until your return."

Odysseus drew back angrily. "What do you mean you moved the bed? I made that bed myself inside our room. I made the frame from seasoned ash, dovetailed the joints, and inlaid the wood with silver, ivory and gold. The bed was far bigger than the door and no one could have moved it out unless they cut it up."

Penelope threw here arms around his neck and kissed and stroked his face in wonder.

"Odysseus, my love, don't be angry with me. No one has moved our bed. I had to be sure it was really you and not some god who'd come to deceive me and steal my love. But now I'm sure of you I could gladly die in your sweet arms."

Tears streamed down both their faces as they embraced. After twenty long years of separation they held each other once again. For a long time they kissed and stared into each other's eyes and said not a word. Then they walked arm in arm to their room, where they found their bed already made up with bowls of fruit and wine laid out beside it. And bright-eyed Athene suspended time that night until they had loved and talked and slept their fill and when at last dawn came, it found them lying happy in each other's arms.

ODYSSEUS
THE KING

News of the suitors' deaths had spread across the city. All night rumour had been rife and by dawn it was confirmed. There was a shocked and stormy gathering in the assembly place. Hundreds of Ithacans had lost relatives or friends.

Eupeithes, father of Antinous, argued passionately for revenge. "Fellow citizens," he declaimed through tears of grief and anger, "look what this king of ours has done to his people. Twenty years ago he left with twelve ships and the flower of Ithacan youth. They were lost to us forever. Now he has returned to kill a second generation; our sons and the sons of our brothers and cousins, left behind when they sailed for Troy. We must avenge them and rid our people of this scourge, Odysseus. Fellow Ithacans, take up your arms and follow me."

It was old Halitherses, friend of Telemachus, who answered him.

"No, my friends, we must not blame Odysseus for the death of these young men. We ourselves are to blame. We let them do as they pleased until they were beyond our control, terrorizing the country and making up their own laws as they went along. And it was the gods who decided they should die. It can do no good to attack Odysseus now. It will only bring more death and suffering and we've suffered enough."

Many of them agreed with these wise words but there were as many others bent upon revenge. Shouting down the rest, they brandished their swords and spears and marched on the palace with Eupeithes at their head. Cries of "Death to Odysseus" echoed through the streets, shattering the early morning peace.

Outside the palace gates Odysseus and Telemachus stood waiting. Athene stood beside them, wrapped in an invisible mist, as they watched the angry mob approach. It was Eupeithes who led the charge. He raised his spear and ran at Odysseus with a bloodcurdling yell. But he never reached him. A sudden thunderbolt came from the sky and struck him to the ground. At once Athene stepped forward out of the mist, dressed in gleaming gold. The Ithacans dropped back in awe.

"Good men of Ithaca, my father Zeus has spoken. Let this death be the last. There's been too much bloodshed in this land. Odysseus has returned and justice has been done. Now you

should make your peace, remember the dead and welcome Odysseus home. And you," said Athene, turning to Odysseus, "should put down your sword, forgive those who forgive you and earn your people's love."

Athene was right. There had already been too much bloodshed. Odysseus went among his people and embraced them, weeping for sorrow and joy. Afterwards, back at the palace, he asked for a great feast of thanksgiving to be prepared. Then he went out, with Penelope beside him, to look for his old father Laertes on his farm in the hills.

They found him bent sadly over his hoe. His garden was well-tended but Laertes himself looked wasted and uncared for. When he saw Odysseus he fainted away and for a moment they thought that the shock had killed him. Happily he soon recovered and, after many tears and fond words, went back with them to the palace.

It was a memorable feast. Most of Ithaca had somehow squeezed into the great hall. There was much sorrow, for so many had died, but there was also great joy, for everyone felt that a time of peace and happiness had come. At long last, after twenty years, Odysseus and Penelope sat together by the fire with their people all around them. There was great wonder too, for after they had eaten and drunk to the gods and the memory of their dead, they clamoured for Odysseus to tell his story. Then they listened spellbound to every adventure, as he told them of the Lotus-Eaters and the Cyclops, of Circe and Hades, of the Sirens and Calypso, of gods and goddesses and of much, much more. It was a story which they would hear again, many, many times and one which they would discuss endlessly among themselves. It was a story to cherish as long as they lived.

Other Kingfisher titles to enjoy

ADVENTURE STORIES
Compiled by Clive King

FUNNY STORIES
Compiled by Michael Rosen

GHOST STORIES
Compiled by Robert Westall

HORSE AND PONY STORIES
Compiled by Christine Pullein-Thompson

MYTHS AND LEGENDS
Retold by Anthony Horowitz

SCHOOL STORIES
Compiled by Jan Mark

SCIENCE FICTION STORIES
Compiled by Edward Blishen